Contemporary Architecture

Made in Germany

D1640988

Contemporary Architecture Made in Germany

Under the auspices of the Federal Chamber of German Architects (BAK) and the Network for Architecture Exchange (NAX), 29 of Germany's leading architectural practices have tackled the challenges of modern global life. They developed potential solutions that they then put into practice within the context of real, existing construction projects. The result is a touring exhibition that, over the next two years, aims to set new milestones in the global architectural discourse. NAX is a growing association of German planners who have achieved international success. We not only facilitate contact between colleagues based in Germany and abroad, but also bring together planners, developers and investors around the world. Here at NAX, we see ourselves as being an active ambassador for the German building culture. As part of this mission, we are regularely present at international trade fairs and events. We are especially pleased that the exhibition has been nominated for the German Design Award 2016. We would like to thank our partner GEZE GmbH, AGC Interpane, JUNG and AIC International who assisted us with the project's realisation. If you would like to know more about the exhibition, including the locations it will be visiting, please visit our website www.nax.bak.de or follow us on Twitter #CONARCGER

CONTEMPORARY
ARCHITECTURE
MADE IN GERMANY
#CONARCGER

Contemporary Architecture
Made in Germany
Worldwide

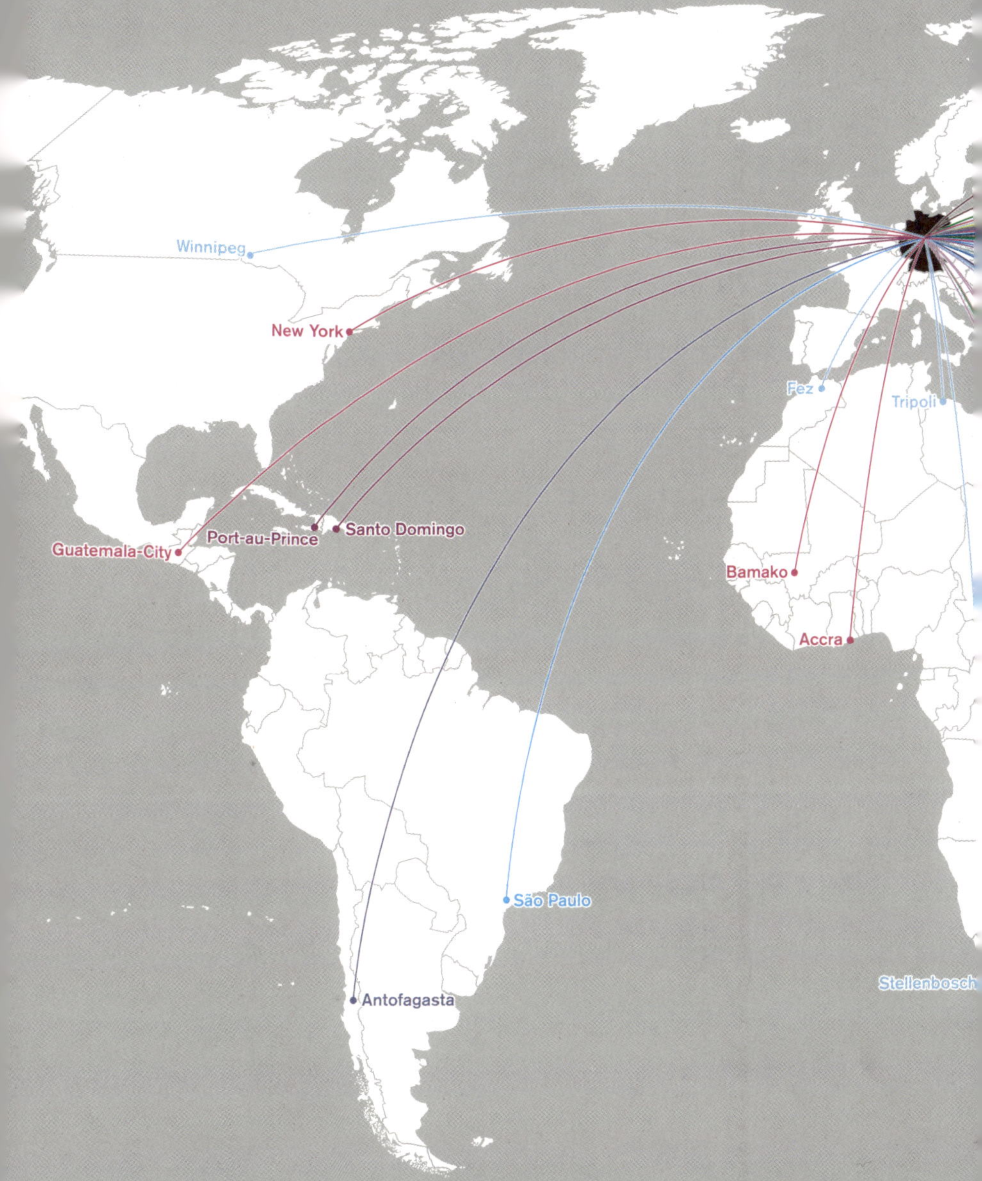

Not all of the projects identified on this map are featured in this book.

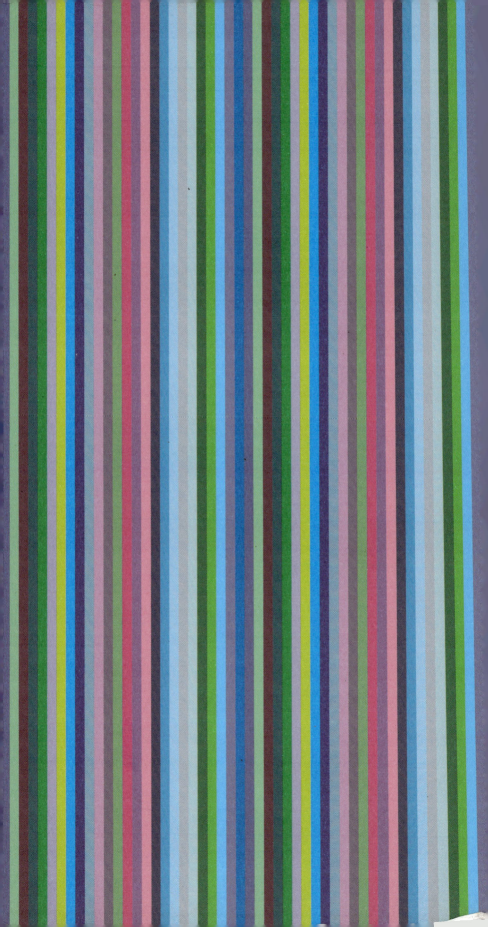

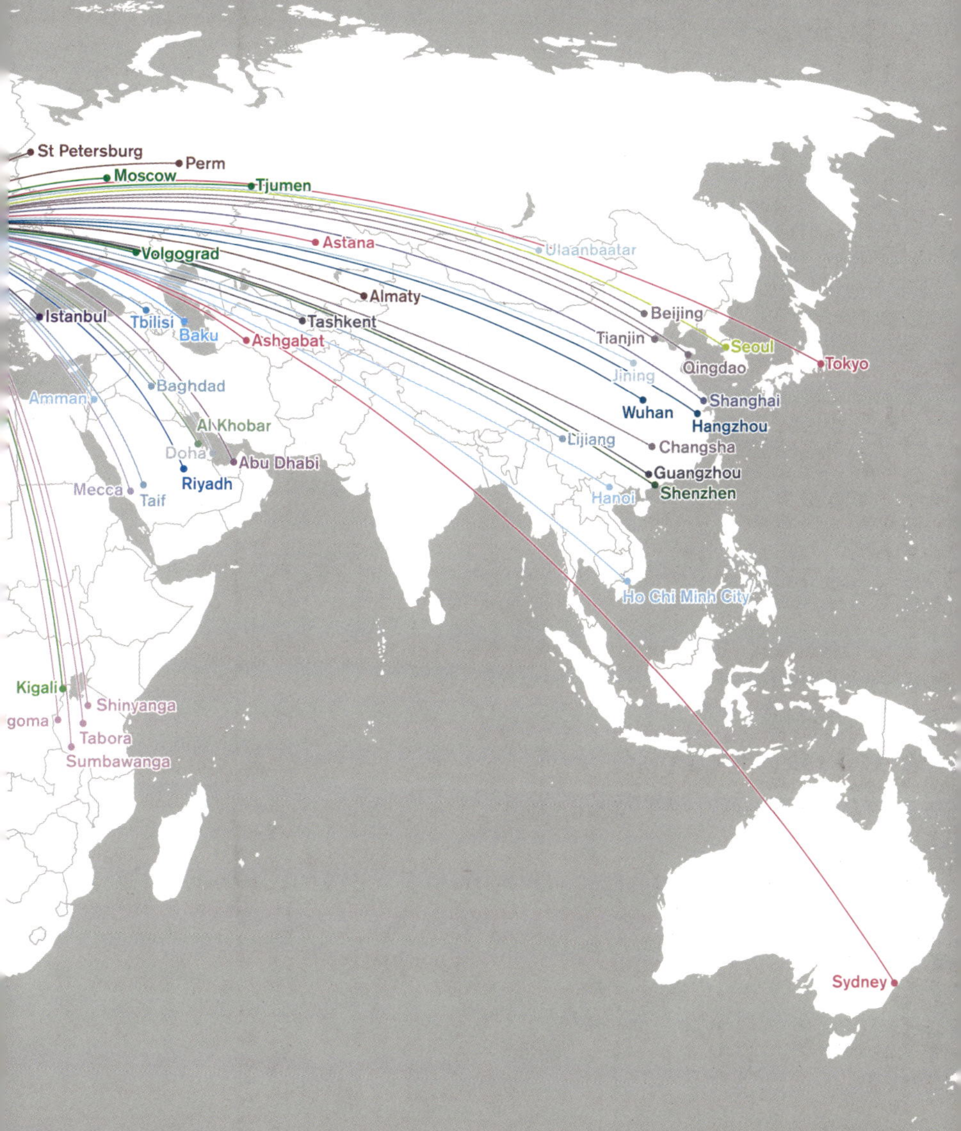

http://goo.gl/v1slQ4

The globalisation of the 21st century has been accompanied by profound economic and social change across all continents. As part of this process, architecture and urban planning are faced with the task of giving a constructional form to these occasionally rapid changes in people's ways of living and working. But global development does not follow one single unified pattern. While the western industrial nations are left to tackle the consequences of demographic change, the emerging and developing nations are faced with industrialisation and urbanisation challenges. Architects and planners capable of meeting the complex demands of the built environment with new ideas and solutions are needed. German architects are in demand across the entire world – both for planning buildings as well as for the conception and implementation of urban development masterplans. With their image as reliable and responsible partners of builders and developers, and an approach to design that values economic efficiency as much as beauty, these architects characterise the brand *Architecture Made in Germany.* This publication uses more than 120 buildings and projects to demonstrate the contemporary achievements of German architects in the following topics:

Metropolis
Developing Urban Structures

Inventing the House of Tomorrow:
Sustainability and Technology

Places for the Public:
Communication, Health, Leisure

Metropolis: Developing Urban Structures

The modern global society is an urban society. With the constant increase in the world's population, the quantity and size of the world's urban areas is also increasing. More than half of the almost 7 billion people on earth currently live in towns and cities. By the year 2050, this proportion will have increased to 69 per cent. At the same time, cities are an economic driver. 80 per cent of the world's gross domestic product is currently created in cities. The process of world urbanisation does not follow a uniform pattern of development, but instead occurs under widely varying conditions. While urban growth in the developed industrial nations goes hand in hand with the development and expansion of modern infrastructure, the material and technical structures in the urban agglomerations of less strongly developed regions of the world develop unsatisfactorily in light of the rapid population growth in those regions. The organisation of sustainable supplies of water and power to those in urban areas, the development of the public space, social welfare, health, protection of the environment and climate, and waste disposal: these are all genuine urban tasks for which city planners and architects worldwide must seek solutions. They give new societal developments a spatial form, whether it be in the design of a building, in an expanding quarter, or as a complex urban concept that offers great quantities of people space for activity and communication.

Pages 25–40

Pages 169–184

Pages 201–216

Pages 329–344

Pages 345–360

Pages 361–376

Pages 377–392

Pages 393–408

Pages 441–456

Left page:
Jining City Culture Center
Jining City, China, RSAA

Inventing the House of Tomorrow: Sustainability and Technology

Protecting the climate and earth's natural resources is a task for the entire society, and therefore urban developers and architects as well. In this context, the use of intelligent technologies plays an especially important role: whether air conditioning, heating, building technology or thermal insulation – the complex interaction of the various energy-related factors must be taken into account in every single planning process. Because, with modern housing technology, it is possible to optimise and reduce the building's energy consumption in a sustainable manner. Simultaneously, innovative building automation systems provide the opportunity to more strongly integrate the architecture with its respective users and their respective needs. However, the sparing and far-sighted use of energy, i.e. our planet's finite resources, does not just begin when a building is put into operation. Even at the planning stage, life-cycle costs must be taken into consideration, as must the question of using materials that can be reutilised or recycled to their maximum potential. Good architecture is more than just the intelligent selection of the right technologies and long-lasting building materials. It integrates the technical and material structures into a design that satisfies the classical architectural criteria: firmitas, utilitas, venustas – strength, utility and beauty.

Pages 57–72

Pages 89–104

Pages 105–120

Pages 153–168

Pages 249–264

Pages 409–424

Pages 425–440

Left page:
Masterplan Harbourcity
Volgograd, Russia, Eller + Eller Architekten

Places for the Public: Communication, Health, Leisure

In any 21st century city that is worth living in, the various social, cultural and economic functions form a tight, multifaceted web. Living, working, leisure, and recreation are no longer separate from each other, but pervade the entire framework of the urban settlement area. City planners and architects take this plurality into consideration, insofar that they allocate certain suitable spaces to these functions, and design them according to the needs and desires of their users. Especially in developing metropolises, where different needs compete for finite space, concepts are required that reconcile the relationship between the public and the private, along with the overlapping urban functions, so that an urban atmosphere can develop. But architecture must also create space for new developments and offerings. Whereas in industrialised countries, a high degree of architectural change is demanded by the profound demographic changes that are occurring. In emerging and developing nations, the need for medical care, educational establishments or stronger industry are the drivers. But both require the same approach: the creative treatment of existing structures on the one hand and typological innovations on the other.

Pages 41–56

Pages 73–88

Pages 121–136

Pages 137–152

Pages 185–200

Pages 217–232

Pages 233–248

Pages 265–280

Pages 281–296

Pages 297–312

Pages 313–328

Pages 457–472

Left page:
Haram Intermodal Station
Mecca, Gerber Architekten

We find that the way and the style of German architects is pure and clean and it belongs to the local architecture.

Khalid Al-Hazzani about Gerber Architekten

Presentation of a German project to King Salman bin Abdulaziz Al Saud, Saudi Arabia

© Ingo Schmitt / Gerber Architekten

GEZE project consulting supports architects, specialist planners, general contractors and clients; from draft planning to beyond project completion – both nationally and internationally.

Brigitte Vöster-Alber, Managing Director of GEZE

As one of the market leaders for door, window and safety technology systems, GEZE provides crucial impulses for building management systems. The company is represented in 130 countries around the world by 31 subsidiaries, 27 of which are outside Germany, by a flexible and highly-efficient sales and service network and by almost 2,600 employees. GEZE has been the main sponsor of the Network for Architecture Exchange (NAX) for many years, and supports architects who operate across borders in developing new markets. With its international team of consultants, GEZE project consulting provides support for architects at home and abroad, during implementation of different building projects. The experts on other countries working at our head office in Leonberg and the project consultants in our worldwide subsidiaries are fully up to speed with local conditions and national building laws. Individual aesthetic concepts and ideas can be realised in conformance with all standards and guidelines. GEZE provides assistance with the development of new ideas and with designing, planning, and tendering, as well as during the implementation phase. Naturally, this includes the devising of all the technically feasible solutions and the coordination of the interfaces with the pre- and post-construction trades every bit as much as the creation of drawings for specific projects, door lists, wiring diagrams and much more besides. The *project* services provided by GEZE are supplemented by events for architects, including seminars and presentations on specific issues of relevance to architects, or on new legal developments. Together with NAX, GEZE also holds informative events for German architects concerning e.g. legal and insurance-related aspects of construction work abroad.

Construction site of German architects in Astana, Kazakhstan

Large panel technology *Made in Germany*

LANXESS

More and more architects are discovering colored concrete as a premium building material. Numerous buildings constructed every year around the world are colored with inorganic pigments from LANXESS.

Rafael Suchan,
Vice President
LANXESS Inorganic
Pigments Asia-Pacific

LANXESS is the world's largest manufacturer of iron oxide pigments and a leading producer of chrome oxides pigments. The color-stable and weather-resistant Bayferrox® and Colortherm® pigments add lasting color to architecture and infrastructure. Over 100 different shades of the individual colors are available. The colors range from yellows to reds, greens and browns, all the way to black. With these products, aesthetic, safe and lasting design effects can be achieved in a wide variety of building materials, such as in-situ concrete, prefabricated concrete components, concrete roofing tiles and paving blocks and even colored asphalt. LANXESS pigments can be used for aesthetic architectural solutions that enable structures to be harmoniously integrated into their environment, or for infrastructure projects that are both functional and creative. For many years now, the LANXESS Colored Concrete Works® initiative has been inspiring architects and construction companies to embrace modern architecture that incorporates colored concrete. Reference projects document its use in international building structures. The initiative is supported by forums and symposiums that provide a platform for architects, construction managers and building companies to exchange ideas and discuss the possibilities of coloring concrete with pigments. Furthermore, LANXESS regularly presents the Colored Concrete Works Award to architects who have distinguished themselves in the innovative use of colored concrete in international projects. All LANXESS products are characterized by a high level of quality and outstanding quality consistency. Due to their outstanding durability and fastness, the color of through-colored concrete pigmented with LANXESS Bayferrox® & Colortherm® pigments will not fade over time. Examples of outstanding buildings in colored concrete from around the world are available on the Internet at www.colored-concrete-works.com.

We appreciate the cooperation with German engineers and architects due to their ability to deliver international competence. The service they are providing is not only technical but cultural as well.

Mahmoud Daen, Arabian Trading & Enterprises, about Meuser Architekten

German architect in Dhahran, Saudi Arabia

Photo: Adrian L. Cross

INTERPANE
Glass for Life

Interpane is specialised in high performance glass products and high end solutions for architecture. We are partners for the consulting right from the beginning of the planning process of each project. With the wide range of products available, our clients increasingly rely on technical advice. Our consultancy-team supports architects, engineers, planners, processors and institutional real estate developers almost all over the world.

Jörn C. Hesselbach, member of the management board

AGC Interpane is one of the major European glass manufacturers and processors, which offers a wide range of functional glass. The company was founded as *Interpane* in Lauenförde (Germany), by Georg F. Hesselbach in 1971. Today it has production facilities at eleven locations in Europe. The product range includes float and low-iron float glass, high-quality coated products for thermal and sound insulation, solar control and safety, glass for interior and exterior-design as well as glass for solar applications. Since mid-2012, AGC Glass Europe and Interpane have a strategic alliance. The glass specialists complement one another, providing an optimised combination of know-how and technology. This has created an outstanding glass portfolio, giving customers across Europe and around the world faster access to products and services. Working together as AGC Interpane, the company now offers its customers a wide range of products with even greater variety – for example a complete range of triple-silver-coated glass products. In addition to the standard temperable, coated float glass, a further strength of the alliance are individual cut-to-size solutions for high-end façades with sophisticated functional glass elements. AGC Interpane also supplies a large number of special solutions upon request. These include specific surface treatments, such as partial coatings and screen printing, as well as customised coatings for unique façade projects. In particular, the alliance produces oversized glass sheets – called *Giga Lites* – for exclusive projects. Float glass coatings up to 18 m (!) in length are possible. Special transport and start-to-end handling complete the range of products and services.

German architect in Sana'a, Yemen

Photo: Muhammad Al-Farabi

German engineers in Bamako, Mali

Photo: Jennifer Tobolla

JUNG

For over 100 years, JUNG has succeeded in expertly forging a link between design standards in terms of material and shape and innovative technology *Made in Germany.* The company stands for comprehensive solutions with a high level of quality – from the development stage, through to the production and finally our customer service.

Harald Jung,
Executive Director

JUNG has been a premium supplier in electrical installation technology for over 100 years. Since its foundation in 1912, this medium-sized family-run company from Schalksmühle in the German Sauerland has established itself as a specialist in switches and systems. Its modern solutions appeal with their ease of use, safety and energy efficiency. The managing directors are Harald Jung, grandson of Albrecht Jung, the company founder, along with Michael Eyrich-Ravens and Martin Herms. JUNG has become an international force to be reckoned with in the industry with 1,200 employees, its own subsidiaries and representation in numerous agencies. The company produces consistently high quality products, which customers rely on throughout the world, at its locations in Schalksmühle and Lünen. JUNG has received the certified *Made in Germany* proof of origin from TÜV NORD for this. Its Insta subsidiary is an electronics technology centre that develops and produces devices and systems for building systems technology in nearby Lüdenscheid. The JUNG portfolio extends from traditional electrical installations and retrofitting by radio right through to networked high-end technology for smart homes. The design aspirations and innovative spirit of the company have been awarded many accolades. The JUNG video and audio indoor stations have most recently received the ICONIC AWARD for Interior Innovation 2016, the flush-mounted LS ZERO switch range has been awarded the Innovation prize for Architecture + Technology 2016 and the classic LS 990 switch – in various different versions – has received the German Design Award 2016. JUNG was also honoured as the Specialist Trade Brand for 2016 – a special distinction of the Plus X Awards.

NAX (Network for Architecture Exchange) is a growing association of German planners who have achieved international success. Under the auspices of the German Federal Chamber of Architects, NAX not only facilitates contact between colleagues based in Germany and abroad, but also brings together planners, developers, and investors around the world. Its successful work is due to, above all, the personal dedication of its members, but also to the support of numerous partners from the political world, economics, and the media. Its common goal: to turn *Architecture Made in Germany* into a global trademark. Also construction companies can benefit from NAX's advice. If they are looking for an experienced planner for their international project, or require background information, they will find that we have expert contact people, make expert recommendations and have useful contacts.

Photo: Christian Kruppa

German architects enjoy an excellent reputation worldwide. Therefore, it is our goal to ensure that architecture *Made in Germany* enjoys a stronger international position.

NAX
NETWORK FOR
ARCHITECTURE
EXCHANGE

NAX Team:
Claudia Sanders,
Gabriele Seitz,
Melanie Läge and
Inga Stein-Barthelmes

AS+P Albert Speer + Partner GmbH

Frankfurt am Main

001
Action Area Plan for Transit-Oriented Development
Riyadh, Saudi Arabia, 2015

After all, Albert Speer and his partners could be considered the green conscience of the sector!

Gerhard Matzig, Süddeutsche Zeitung

Visualisation: Peter Tjie, emptyform

AS+P play a considerable role in the comprehensive urban restructuring and modernisation of the Saudi Arabian capital Riyadh, providing numerous concepts. The planned public transport system is intended to take the metropolis' traffic and urban development to a new infrastructural level. In order to present an alternative to car transport, currently the dominant transportation mode, it is not only necessary to provide an efficient bus and train system, but also a qualitatively upgraded urban space, which is welcoming and provides a high quality of life. For the existing sensitive urban fabric of Riyadh's historic center, AS+P presented a strategy, the Action Area Plan for Transit-Oriented Development (T.O.D.). Its aim was not only the optimisation and integration of transport routes and transportation modes, in a way compatible with the urban environment, but also to take into account the cultural and historical importance of the old city centre. Based on the vision of a Capital Oasis, over the next 25 years Riyadh's centre will ripen into an open, varied place, comprising architectural treasures, representative squares and buildings plus a network of differentiated roads and transport connections, which will form the physical framework of a modern, vibrant urban fabric.

001

Action Area Plan for Transit-Oriented Development

Riyadh, Saudi Arabia, 2015

Visualisation : Peter Tjie, emptyform

17 NORTH EAST LOOP

002

Fraport AG Headquarters

Frankfurt am Main Airport, Germany, 2013

Photo: Uwe Dettmar

002
Fraport AG Headquarters
Frankfurt am Main Airport, Germany, 2013

Photo: Uwe Dettmar

INFO

003
Criminal Court Complex
Riyadh, Saudi Arabia, 2014

Photo: ADA – Arriyadh Development Authority

003
Criminal Court Complex
Riyadh, Saudi Arabia, 2014

Photo: ADA – Arriyadh Development Authority

AS+P Albert Speer + Partner GmbH

Office Frankfurt am Main
Hedderichstrasse 108-110
60596 Frankfurt am Main – Germany
+49.69.605011-0
mail@as-p.de

Office Shanghai
225 Xikang Road
200040 Shanghai – China
+86.21.31267881
info@as-p-china.com.cn
www.as-p.de

Photo: Uwe Dettmar

AS+P draw upon more than 50 years of worldwide planning and building expertise. Thanks to their ideas, plans and projects, they can be regarded as being one of the most innovative planning offices in operation today. Their comprehensive, multifaceted portfolio shows that AS+P are generalists but with specialist knowledge in virtually all planning disciplines. Their projects range from building construction, urban planning, urban and regional development to landscape architecture, leisure and tourism planning, conceptual transport planning and project management, right up to planning-specific preparation of major events and expert opinions for policy advising. The architectural and planning practice currently employs around 180 professionals. AS+P regard their international involvement as being not just a chance to export German knowhow, but also to use the experience that they accumulate in foreign countries as a resource from which projects at other locations can profit.

Auer Weber
Munich

004
Buildings in the Botanical Garden
Shanghai, China, 2010

Shanghai's new botanical garden was created in a local recreation area for the occasion of the EXPO 2010. It was embedded into the existing topography, which includes a 70 m-high hill, and stretches out across an area of 200 ha. Its architectural framework forms a modelled garden ring, which also comprises the entrance building, spacious greenhouses, and a research centre. Thanks to their well-thought out placement and forms that are orientated towards their environment, the biomorphic buildings blend into the hilly landscape in an almost symbiotic manner. Viewed from a distance, the concrete and glass take on scenic qualities, so that their reflective shells correspond to the lakes and the interplay of daylight. The subtle reference to the surrounding nature is also apparent in the detail: the delicate roof construction is reminiscent of the microscopic structure of a leaf or piece of fabric. Furthermore, in their lightness, and surrounded by greenery, the buildings reference the architecture of the pavilions and temporary buildings.

Photo: Roland Halbe

Photo: Roland Halbe

004
Buildings in the Botanical Garden
Shanghai, China, 2010

Be it a prestigious or a supposedly unremarkable project, there are always new architectural answers to be discovered, which not only display a great variety of forms, but also have one thing in common: they require a detailed analysis of the location and its requirements, as well as thorough understanding of the cultural context and needs of the users.

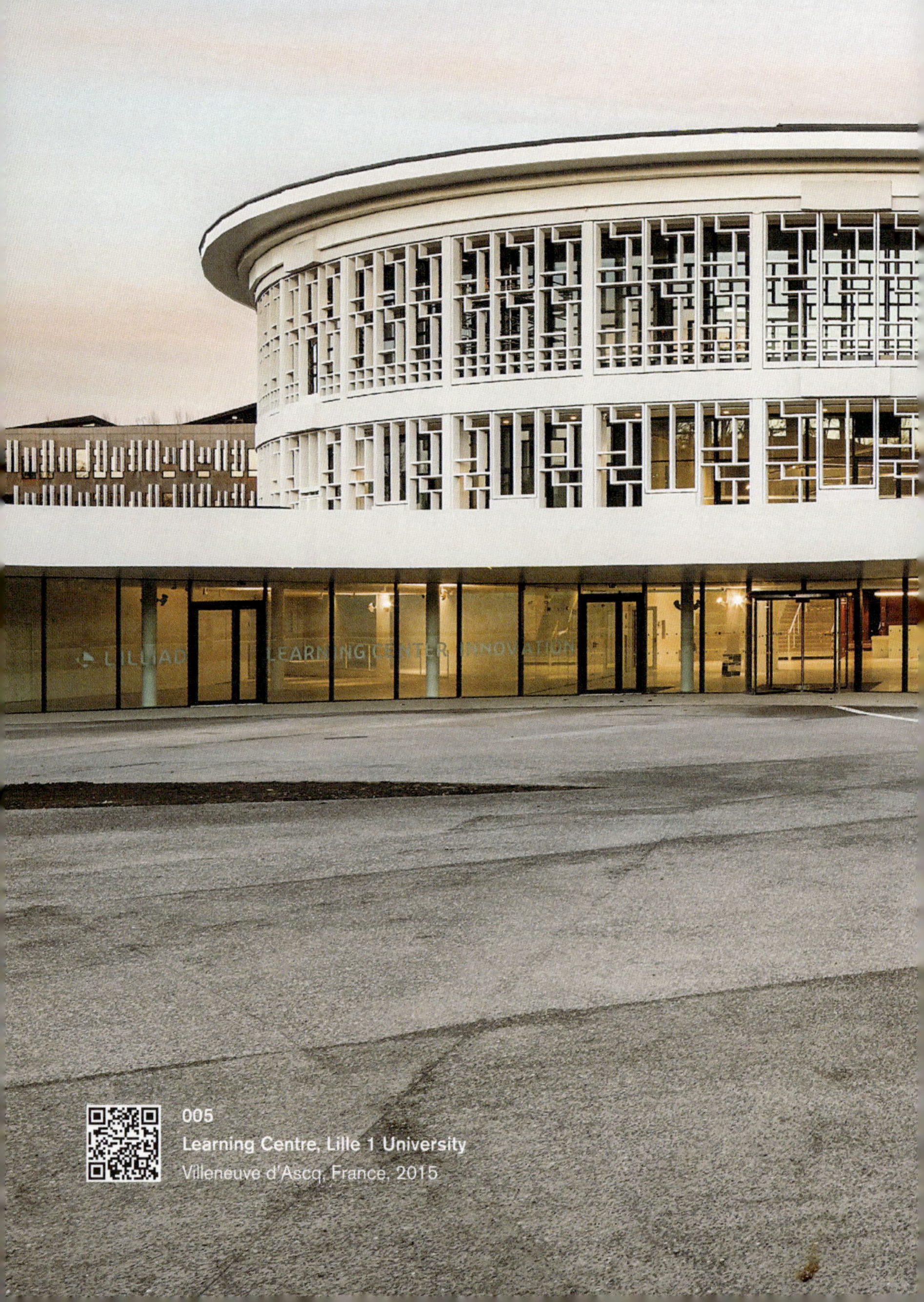

005
Learning Centre, Lille 1 University
Villeneuve d'Ascq, France, 2015

Photo: Aldo Amoretti

006
Azur Arena Antibes
Antibes, France, 2013

Photo: Aldo Amoretti

007

ESO Hotel Cerro Paranal

Antofagasta, Chile, 2002

Photo: Roland Halbe

008

Aquamotion Aquatic Centre

Courchevel, France, 2015

Photo: Aldo Amoretti

Auer Weber

Auer Weber, the multiple award-winning practice founded in 1980, specialises in the conception, redesign, conversion, and renovation of commercial premises and public buildings. This internationally experienced business employs a staff of 140 at its premises in Munich and Stuttgart. The practice's architecture stems from an intensive involvement with the construction project itself, along with the conditions and potential of the place where it will be built. The resulting drafts range from sculpturally formed free-standing buildings, to urban planning.

Office Stuttgart
Haussmannstrasse 103 A
70188 Stuttgart – Germany
+49.711.268404-0
stuttgart@auer-weber.de

Office Munich
Sandstrasse 33
80335 Munich – Germany
+49.89.381617-0
muenchen@auer-weber.de

www.auer-weber.de

Photo: Marc Schäfer

Bollinger + Grohmann Ingenieure

Frankfurt am Main

Thanks to its spiry design, the new construction of the European Central Bank in Frankfurt thrusts into the skyline of the financial metropolis, where it seeks a connection to the high-rise buildings of the private financial institutions. But it's a gesture of space: because when all's said and done, we are talking about the financial institution for all European citizens. Architects from the Austrian Coop Himmelb(l)au agency have expressed this self-conception in the form of two towers, which extend in full height above a glazed atrium. The two striking towers, 185 and 165 m-tall, are connected to each other via walkways, ramps, steel struts, and reinforced concrete floors, thus giving the impression of being one single entity. Another exceptional constructional challenge that faced the engineers was the integration of the listed market hall in the grounds of the new building. The 220 m-long, 52 m-wide brick building was carefully restored. As part of this, the restoration concept was created in close cooperation with the authorities responsible for listed buildings. Today, the large market hall provides the main entrance to the high-rise structure on its northern side, and apart from the lobby, primarily hosts conference rooms and the ECB's press centre.

009 European Central Bank
Coop Himmelb(l)au
Frankfurt am Main, Germany, 2014

Photo: Paul Raftery

009 European Central Bank
Coop Himmelb(l)au
Frankfurt am Main, Germany, 2014

Photo: Paul Raftery

Photo: DC Towers / Michael Nagl

Since the practice was founded by Klaus Bollinger and Manfred Grohmann in 1983, we have been driven by our passion for good architecture and innovative construction. As responsible engineers, our focus is on strengthening and developing the respective individual draft. We regard ourselves as being partners in an interdisciplinary planning team and develop custom solutions together with architects and developers, construction firms, the construction industry, as well as the relevant specialist planners. These are always an integral component of the overall concept and never created as an end in themselves.

010 Vienna DC Tower
Dominique Perrault Architecture
Vienna, Austria, 2014

Photo: Christian Richters

011 King Fahad National Library
Gerber Architekten
Riyadh, Saudi Arabia, 2013

012 Louvre Lens
SANAA, Kazuyo Sejima & Ryue Nishizawa
Lens, France, 2012

Photo: Iwan Baan

GUIDES MULTIMÉDIA
MULTIMEDIA GUIDES
MULTIMEDIAGIDSEN

Photo: Roland Halbe

012 Louvre Lens
SANAA, Kazuyo Sejima & Ryue Nishizawa
Lens, France, 2012

Klaus Bollinger and
Manfred Grohmann

Bollinger + Grohmann Ingenieure

Engineering achievements are often not noticeable to those viewing buildings, but without them, there would be no houses or buildings. It reflects well on engineers if their work allows the architecture itself to shine. It is in this sense that the Bollinger + Grohmann Ingenieure practice has come to regard itself. Its solutions in the fields of structure planning, façade planning, construction physics, and fire prevention always strengthen and build upon the respective architectural drawings provided. Staff at this practice, founded in 1983, regard themselves as being partners in an interdisciplinary planning team and develop custom solutions, together with architects and developers, along with the relevant trades and specialist planners. These begin with the drafts and come to form an integral component of the overall concept. In dialogue, plans come into being, which transform even the boldest architectural ideas into projects that are technically and economically realisable, without surrendering an iota of their creative ideas.

Photo: FAZ, Frank Röth

Braun Schlockermann Dreesen
Frankfurt am Main

013

Vesnovka, Multifunctional Residential Complex

Almaty, Kazakhstan, 2014

In Almaty, the former capital of Kazakhstan, situated at the foot of the Tian Shan mountain range, a building complex was constructed on a parcel of land of 20,000 m^2. The practice was responsible for the architectural plans, the façade planning, and the overall creative management. Due to the city's location in an earthquake prone area, the structural planning for this project was especially designed for that issue. This complex of buildings, of various heights and with subtly protruding individual buildings, provided for flats as well as office space, retail units and restaurants created a new sub centre in the city of Almaty. Upon close inspection, the complex's lively roof ridge line really stands out, largely thanks to its unusual roof shape: it borrows from the traditional head covering born by Kazakh men.

БАНК
СПОРТ
СПОРТ
АПТЕКА
МАГАЗИН

Whether in Nigeria or Kazakhstan … the personal contact with the client and our presence on site is the key to understanding the complexity of structural building processes and their local and cultural background.

For being able to incorporate the different needs and requirements into our work, we see it as our obligation to ensure comprehensive and responsible solutions. Therefore our team consists of people with ideas that create values!

013
Vesnovka, Multifunctional Residential Complex
Almaty, Kazakhstan, 2014

014
Business park with Hotel Perm
Perm, Russia, 2018

015
Football stadium
St. Petersburg, Russia (Competition)

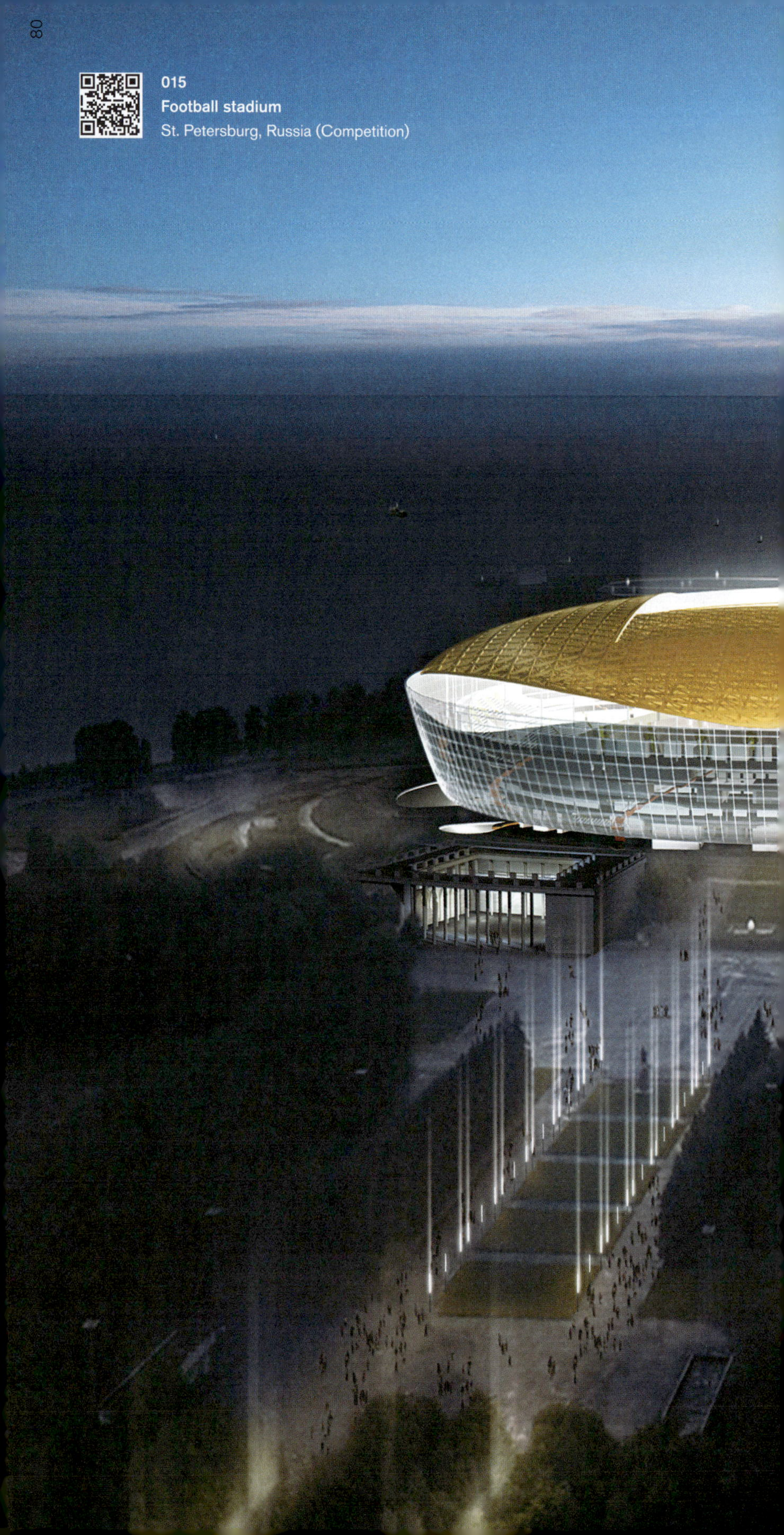

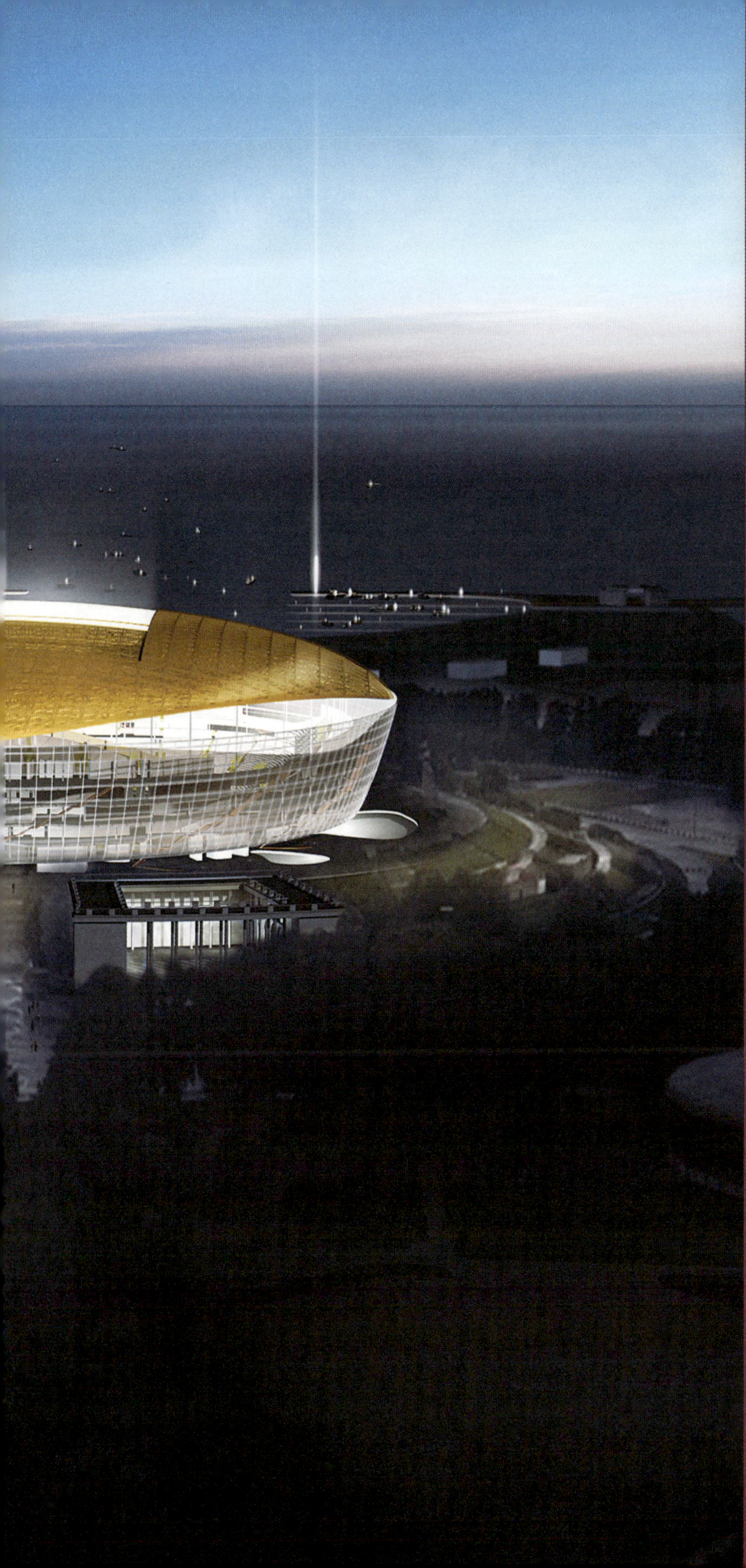

016

Marina Towers

St. Petersburg, Russia (Competition)

017

Archives of the Russian Academy of Sciences

St Petersburg, Russia, 2015

Российская академия наук осуществляет свою деятельность в целях обеспечения преемственности и координации фундаментальных научных исследований и поисковых
Архив Российской академии наук

адемия наук осуществляет свою деятельность в целях
преемственности и координации фундаментальных
едований и поисковых научных исследований,
о важнейшим направлениям естественных, технических,
сельскохозяйственных, общественных и гуманитарных
ного научного обеспечения деятельности органов
ной власти, научно-методического руководства научной и
ческой деятельностью научных организаций и
ных организаций высшего образования.
осуществляет свою деятельность в целях
ординации фундаментальных

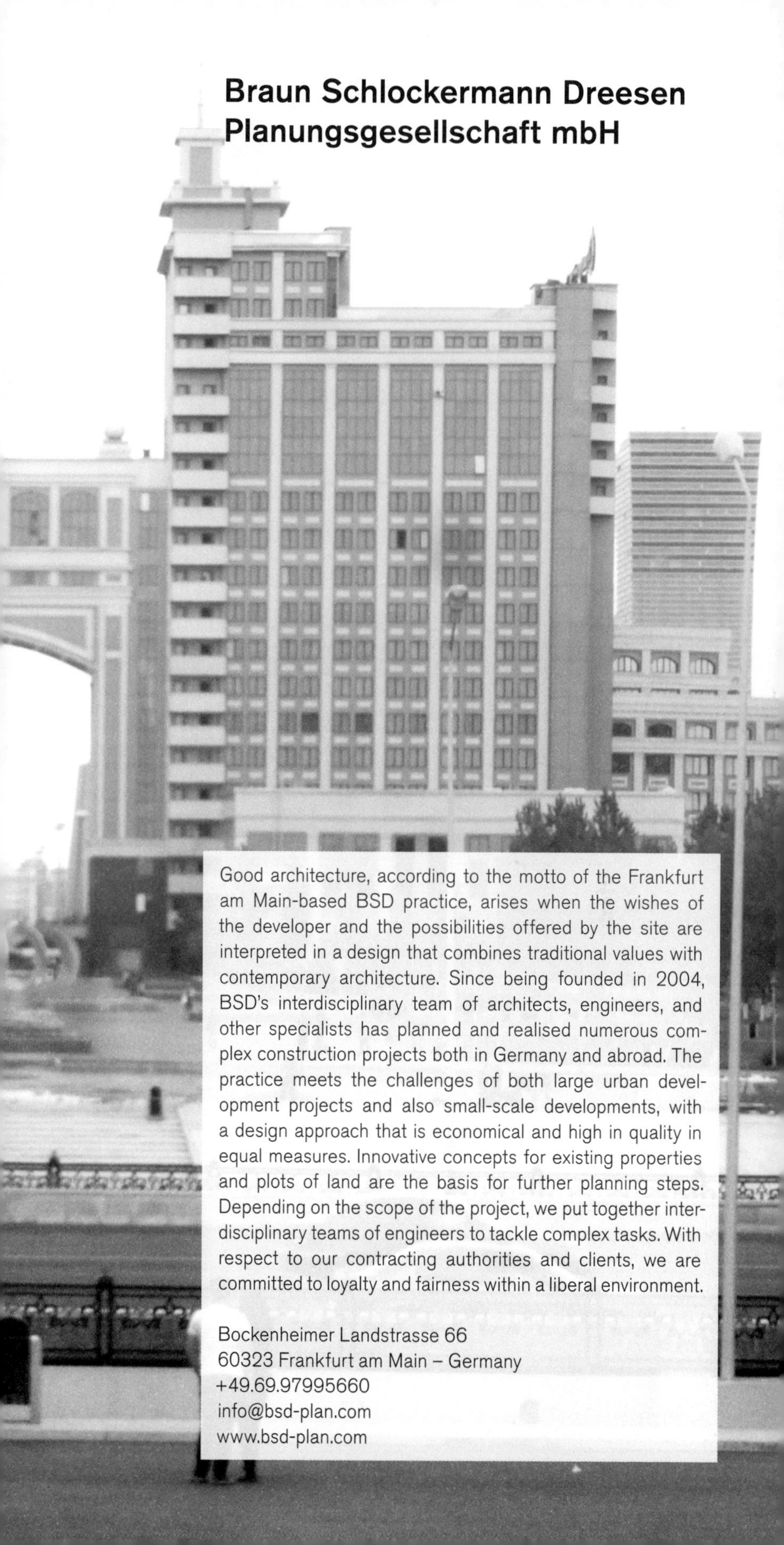

Braun Schlockermann Dreesen Planungsgesellschaft mbH

Good architecture, according to the motto of the Frankfurt am Main-based BSD practice, arises when the wishes of the developer and the possibilities offered by the site are interpreted in a design that combines traditional values with contemporary architecture. Since being founded in 2004, BSD's interdisciplinary team of architects, engineers, and other specialists has planned and realised numerous complex construction projects both in Germany and abroad. The practice meets the challenges of both large urban development projects and also small-scale developments, with a design approach that is economical and high in quality in equal measures. Innovative concepts for existing properties and plots of land are the basis for further planning steps. Depending on the scope of the project, we put together interdisciplinary teams of engineers to tackle complex tasks. With respect to our contracting authorities and clients, we are committed to loyalty and fairness within a liberal environment.

Bockenheimer Landstrasse 66
60323 Frankfurt am Main – Germany
+49.69.97995660
info@bsd-plan.com
www.bsd-plan.com

Eike Becker_Architekten
Berlin

The ma|ro ensemble is a pair of buildings that form a gateway to the Neue Rothofstrasse in the centre of Frankfurt am Main. The designers deliberately eschewed an identical design for these kindred structures. Although both buildings are easily recognisable as being interrelated, the actual distance between them is highlighted in the diverse arrangement of the various layers that form the façade. A concept based on stacking and shifting frames is responsible for the angular and irregular contours. Enclosures protrude from the main façade into the public space and create a sense of vibrant movement within the orthogonal massing. A transparent curtain wall is accentuated by projections and mediates between the adjacent buildings with their rather traditional townhouse architecture and the shiny and sleek banking towers so typical of this metropolis on the Main River.

018
ma|ro Office and Business Premises
Frankfurt am Main, Germany, 2016

018
ma|ro Office and Business Premises
Frankfurt am Main, Germany, 2016

We find ourselves in the midst of a monsoon of polymorphic demands and specific knowledge. Superimposing these different levels brings about interferences. Escalations of this experience – which we termed *superference* – became our architectural method of design.

019
Wye
Neuss, Germany, 2007

020
4Cubes, Highrise N3 Končar
Split, Croatia, 2018

021
Zair
Zagreb, Croatia, 2019

021
Zair
Zagreb, Croatia, 2019

Eike Becker_Architekten

Because urban architecture is by its very nature also urban design, every designer of a new building also takes on the responsibility for the neighbourhood in which it is built. This may be the most precise definition of the philosophy and self-regard of Eike Becker Architects. Since being founded in 1999, the practice has predominately produced designs for dense urban environments. Its services span from office and administrative buildings through high rises and hotels to multiunit housing, and right up to complex urban design projects. Its projects are always developed for their specific context, and imbue prominent locations with a new face, or come to redefine urban spaces. The planners reconcile timely relevance, in the sense of innovative technology, energy efficiency and sustainability, with the classic ideal of the European city.

Jean-Monnet-Strasse 2
10557 Berlin – Germany
+49.30.2593740
info@eb-a.de

Eller + Eller Architekten
Düsseldorf

022

FGS Campus – Flick Gocke Schaumburg

Bonn, Germany, 2016

The design of a new headquarters for the Flick Gocke Schaumburg auditing company in Bonn follows the priorities of a contemporary working environment: flexibility, communication and focus. For the company's 750 employees, we developed a building that combines the openness of a campus with efficient spatial organisation, and a design that helps build up identity. The communicative areas, comprising meeting rooms, a library, an exhibition area, a fitness centre, and a cafe are found in the ground floor, while the upper storeys are used as a flexibly dimensioned office space. The four-winged structure, with its trapezoidal floor plan, forms a light, open atrium, which provides atmospheric advantages that benefit the four inward-projecting transparent office sections. But the building's inner transparency also provides a valuable urban planning benefit: its transparent, dynamic façade brings light and movement to the streetscape.

022
FGS Campus – Flick Gocke Schaumburg
Bonn, Germany, 2016

023
Headquarters BASF
Ludwigshafen, Germany, 2019

024
Research- and Development Center TMK
Skolkovo, Russia, 2014

For 50 years now, we have been engaged in the effectiveness of architecture and the opportunities it presents to advance society.

Photo: Werner Huthmacher

025
Fünf Morgen Dahlem Urban Village
Berlin, Germany, 2014

026
Residential Campus
Tjumen, Russia, 2018

027

Masterplan Harbourcity

Volgograd, Russia, 2012

Eller + Eller Architekten

The Eller + Eller Architekten practice, founded in 1964, designs spaces and buildings in which people's aspirations are the central focus. The aim of the dedicated, future-orientated team, with offices in Düsseldorf, Berlin and Moscow, is to create vibrant, efficient buildings that are characterised by high levels of responsibility: both socially and from an architectural-cultural perspective. Eller + Eller Architekten's range of services encompasses building projects of all sizes and types: urban masterplans and complex structural contexts, but also single structures and interior design. Eller + Eller Architekten therefore see themselves as having a duty of responsibility towards the client and to society, which spans from the very first drafts, elaborate technical and design details, through turnkey management, and the development of complex, large-scale projects.

Office Düsseldorf
Augustastrasse 30
40477 Düsseldorf – Germany
+49.211.4352-0
duesseldorf@eller-eller.de

Office Berlin
Friedrichstrasse 210
10969 Berlin – Germany
+49.30.616703-0
berlin@eller-eller.de

Office Moscow
ul. Petrovka 27
107031 Moscow – Russia
+7.495.2236391
moscow@eller-eller.de

www.eller-eller.de

Photo: Till Budde

Falk von Tettenborn Architekten

Munich

028
Hotel Montana
Pétion-Ville, Haiti, 2017

Two hotel projects in the Caribbean – a new-build in Haiti along with the conversion of a historical building in the neighbouring Dominican Republic – serve as examples of the practice's integrative approach to creating designs. After the Hotel Montana, which sits on a hilltop in Haiti's capital Port-au-Prince, was destroyed in the 2010 earthquake, an architectural competition was launched to rebuild it. The winning entry preserved the art deco character that the traditional hotel had boasted since its construction in 1946. In form and design, the buildings and open air facilities take on the character of the lavish tropical environment, and seem to blend into the topography and vegetation. Thanks to its utilisation of the natural wind direction, along with modern building techniques such as a cooling component, in the form of tempered concrete ceilings, it wasn't necessary to install an air conditioning system. The renovation and conversion of a former convent school in the historical centre of Santo Domingo in the Dominican Republic also demonstrates great sensitivity towards the building as it previously existed. The architectural remnants of the colonial era remain, but were carefully extended with what are recognisable as new, modern structures.

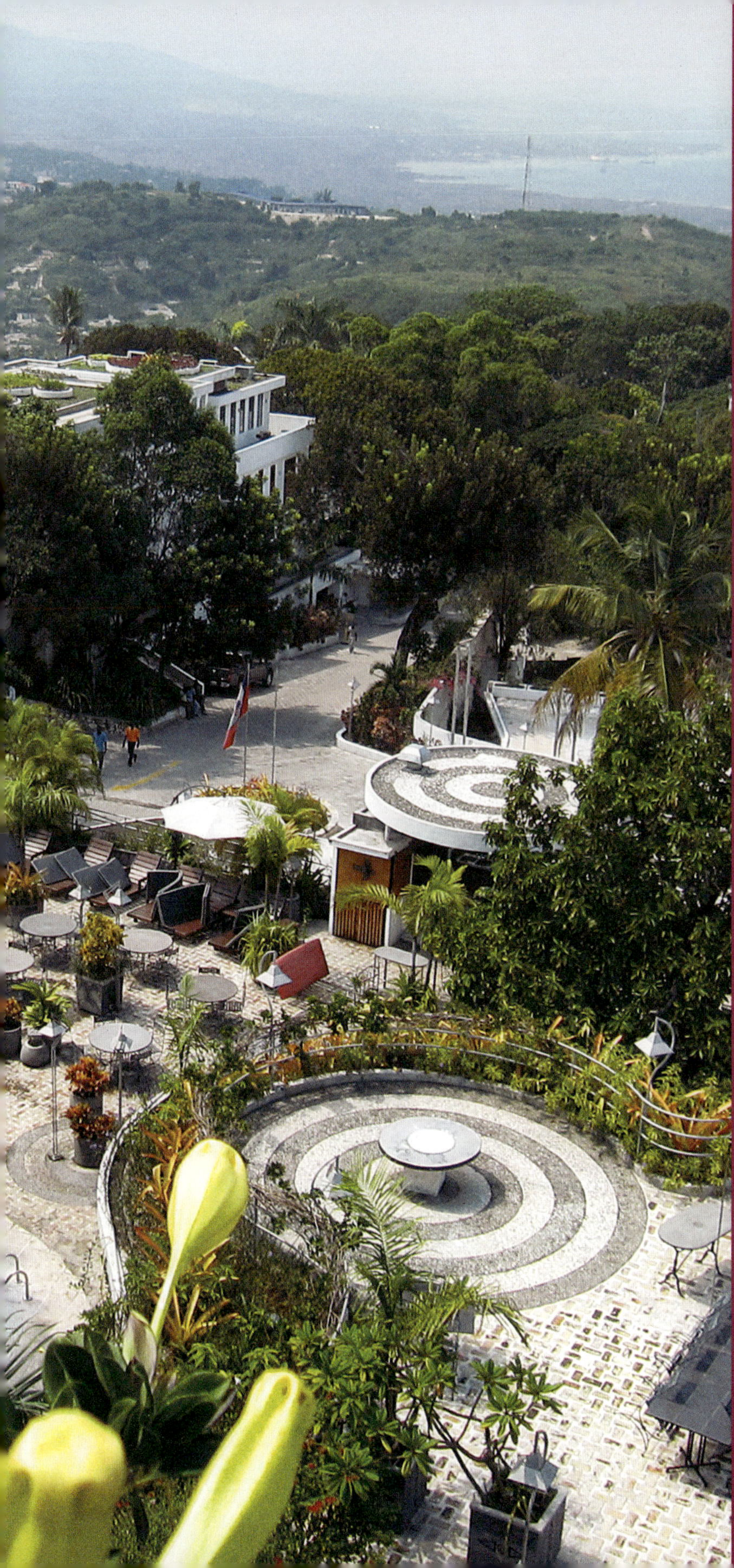

029
Hotel Billini
Santo Domingo, Dominican Republic, 2014

030
NuOffice
Munich, Germany, 2015

Photo: Walter Wohlrab

A city worth living in must not only be composed of intelligent construction methods and smart utilisation concepts, but also imaginative buildings! Our buildings are designed to provide nourishment for the soul, even on dull rainy days!

Photo: Walter Wohlrab

030
NuOffice
Munich, Germany, 2015

031
Water Tower Hamburg
Hamburg, Germany, 2007

Photo: Aloys Kiefer

031
Water Tower Hamburg
Hamburg, Germany, 2007

Photo: Aloys Kiefer

Falk von Tettenborn Architekten & Innenarchitekten

The Falk von Tettenborn practice in Munich can draw upon more than 30 years' experience in the design and construction of very distinct residential and office buildings, along with hotels. The drafts show an approach that understands that the manifest building structure serves as a framework and prerequisite for the interior architecture. The architecture of the individual projects fits into local conditions without relinquishing the requirement to be something special. A good example of this would be the water tower in Hamburg that was turned into an exclusive hotel. With the aid of the very latest construction methods, it was possible to breathe new life into this industrial monument while at the same time preserving the historical structure and surrounding park. The choice of materials, shapes and the integration of nature, bears witness to this quest to combine sensory qualities with urban planning expertise and architectural class. The practice can rely on the support of an extensive network of specialists, and is experienced in dealing with local authorities; not just in Europe but also in other places of the world.

Grüntenstrasse 22
80686 Munich – Germany
+49.89.5177710
post@tettenborn.net
www.tettenborn.net

Gerber Architekten
Dortmund

032
King Fahad National Library
Riyadh, Saudi Arabia, 2014

The King Fahad National Library in Riyadh was the result of the winning entry in an international competition. The building acknowledges thousands of years of old scholarly tradition in the Arabian region, while at the same time interpreting the construction styles that are typical in the region as a piece of contemporary architecture. The converted and respectfully preserved existing building – the old library – not only forms the core of the new library in the material sense, but also fulfils this role in its new function as stack room. The glass façade of the rectangular-shaped new building is enwrapped by a tightly stretched sail construction, manufactured with a pale fabric. This not only references the Arab tent tradition, but also protects the interior from solar radiation. The construction of the library succeeds in linking the requirements of restructuring the urban environment with contemporary architecture, and the creation of a public space.

Photo: Christian Richters

032
King Fahad National Library
Riyadh, Saudi Arabia, 2014

Photo: Christian Richters

Photo: Christian Richters

032
King Fahad National Library
Riyadh, Saudi Arabia, 2014

033

Butterfly Dome

Riyadh, Saudi Arabia, 2020

034

Haram Intermodal Station

Mecca, Saudi Arabia, Design 2013

We take our clients' individual requirements and develop these further while integrating both the functionality and the particularities of each project.

035
Info.HUB
Riyadh, Saudi Arabia, 2021

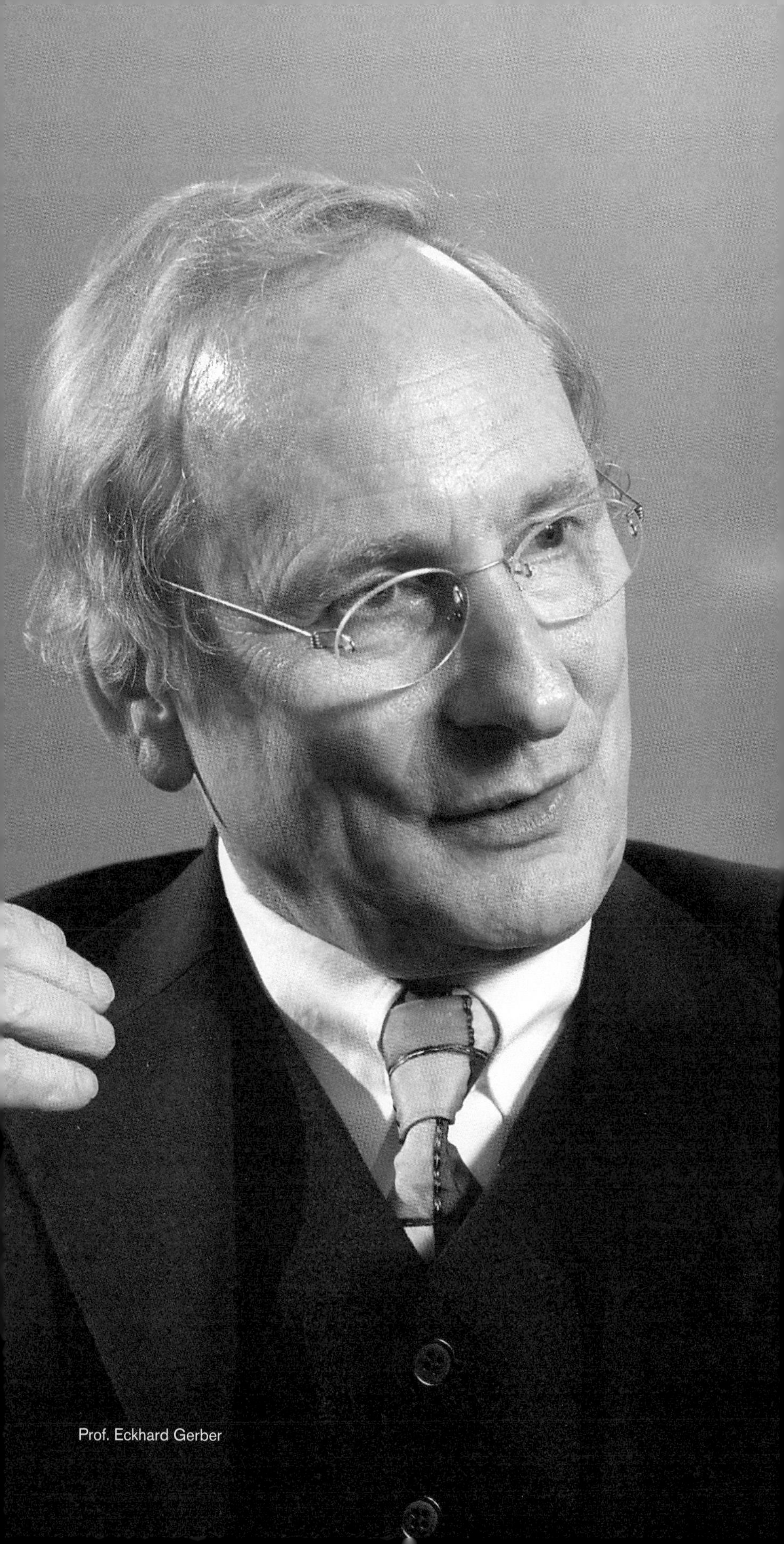
Prof. Eckhard Gerber

Gerber Architekten

The Gerber Architekten practice is active throughout the world and can look back on nearly 50 years of experience in urban planning, landscape architecture, architecture, and interior design. The 170 staff members' expertise ranges from office blocks, to buildings for academic and cultural institutions, right up to housing construction. Internationally, Gerber Architekten is predominantly active in the Middle East and in China. The practice has not only its head office in Dortmund but branch offices in Hamburg, Berlin, Riyadh, and Shanghai. The architectural plans are always geared to the specific conditions of the respective site, its history and topography, combining visionary, contemporary architecture with energy-saving, ecological parameters.

Tönnishof 9-13
44149 Dortmund – Germany
+49.231.9065-0
kontakt@gerberarchitekten.de
www.gerberarchitekten.de

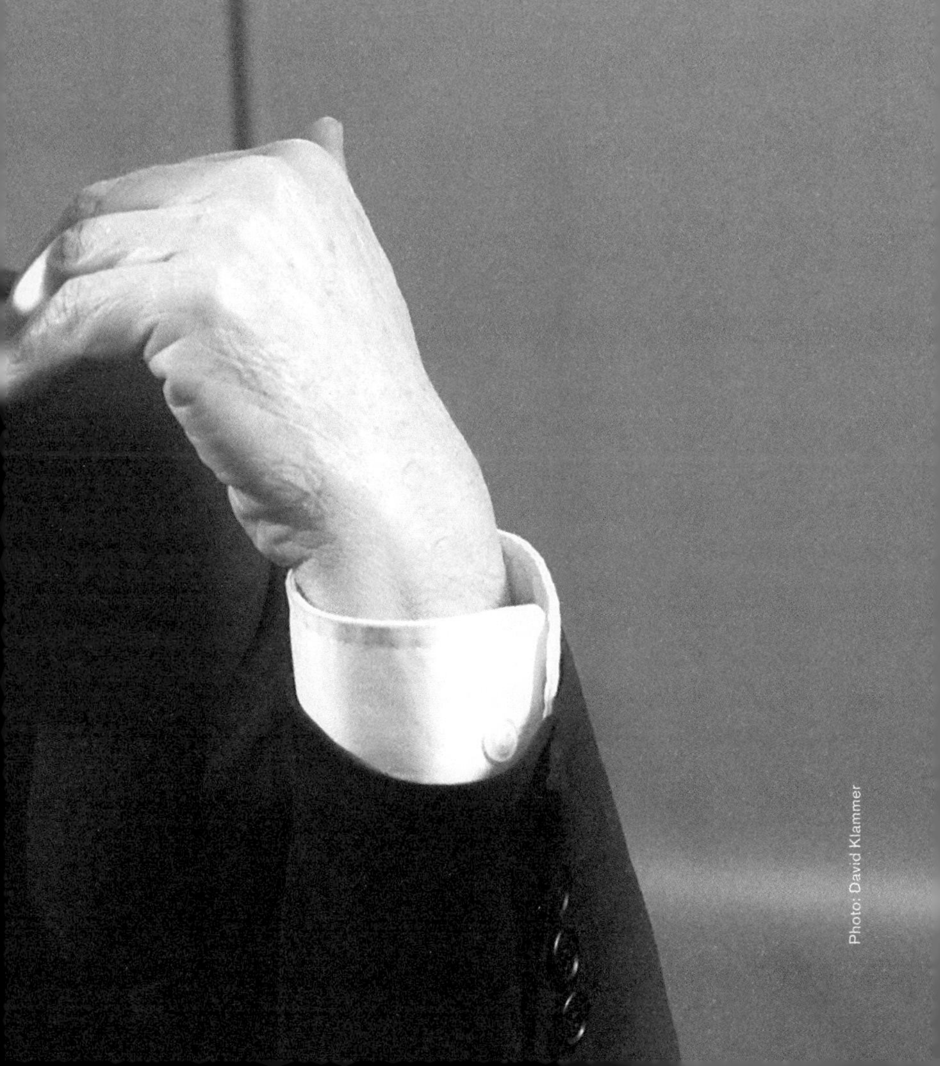

Photo: David Klammer

GRAFT Architekten
Berlin

036

Holistic living energy-plus houses

Berlin, Germany, 2014

Photo: Tobias Hein

The agency was responsible for the design of three new energy-plus buildings in Berlin. These are buildings that generate more energy than is required for their own running and for supplying the inhabitants. The trio of buildings comprises a detached property and two terrace houses, and distinguishes itself by the exclusive use of sustainable, sound building materials, innovative, and highly efficient housing technology plus a complementary electro-mobility concept. This holistic approach, which takes into consideration not only the building's consumption levels and energy requirements, but also the everyday lives and practice of its occupants, also takes into account the finite nature of all architecture. So at the end of their lifetime, the building materials used can be reused or disposed of in an environmentally friendly manner. This commendable, yet in the best sense of the word, modest, concept combines the design with an expressive architectonic gesture and an intelligent room layout. In this concept, the light, outward-facing areas and areas for private retreat are harmoniously organised.

037
Old Mill Hotel Radisson Blu
Belgrade, Serbia, 2015

Photo: Tobias Hein

OLD MILL BELGRADE

038
Autostadt Roof and Service Pavilion
Wolfsburg, Germany, 2013

Photo: Tobias Hein

039
Paragon Apartments
Berlin, Germany, 2016

Photo: Tobias Hein

040

Family House Sankt Augustin

Sankt Augustin, Germany, 2014

Photo: Jan Kraege

RONALD McDONALD HAUS
SANKT AUGUSTIN

041 / 042

Platoon Kunsthalle

Berlin, Germany and Seoul, South Korea, 2012

Photo: platoon.org

9
P

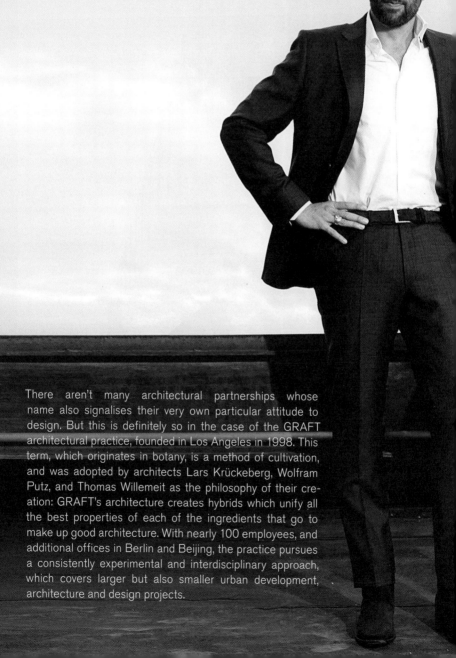

GRAFT
Gesellschaft von Architekten mbH

Heidestrasse 50
10557 Berlin – Germany
+49.30.306451030
pr@graftlab.com
www.graftlab.com

There aren't many architectural partnerships whose name also signalises their very own particular attitude to design. But this is definitely so in the case of the GRAFT architectural practice, founded in Los Angeles in 1998. This term, which originates in botany, is a method of cultivation, and was adopted by architects Lars Krückeberg, Wolfram Putz, and Thomas Willemeit as the philosophy of their creation: GRAFT's architecture creates hybrids which unify all the best properties of each of the ingredients that go to make up good architecture. With nearly 100 employees, and additional offices in Berlin and Beijing, the practice pursues a consistently experimental and interdisciplinary approach, which covers larger but also smaller urban development, architecture and design projects.

Photo: Ali Kepenek

HPP Architects
Düsseldorf

043
Vodafone Campus
Düsseldorf, Germany, 2012

Photo: Ralph Richter

043
Vodafone Campus
Düsseldorf, Germany, 2012

Photo: Ralph Richter

The Vodafone Campus in Düsseldorf, capital of the German North Rhine-Westphalia state, was constructed on the site of a former brewery. The newly built headquarters of the communication business, in the form of a closed campus, provides working space for approximately 5,500 employees. A particular challenge was to ensure that the new buildings were integrated into the existing urban context, without the campus being sealed off from the neighbouring residential area. The area was therefore created as a consistent urban quarter, containing a public park, and featuring restaurants and cafes in the new buildings' ground floors. The buildings' architecture reflects the client's self-image: communicative, dynamic and innovative.

044
Shopping center Hofgarten
Solingen, Germany, 2013

Photo: Jens Willebrand

045

Clariant Innovation Center

Frankfurt am Main, Germany, 2013

Photo: Sigurd Steinprinz

046
Dreischeibenhaus
Düsseldorf, Germany, 2014

Photo: MOMENI Gruppe

Our architecture is defined by the undogmatic examination of a project's particular topics, not by continuous application of identical formal arrangements independent from task and location. In doing so, we are following an integrated work approach, starting from the urban requirements, the constructional and cultural context as well as the function of each building typology.

047

AND

Istanbul, Turkey, 2015

Photo: Onur Gurkan

HPP Architects

Kaistrasse 5
40221 Düsseldorf – Germany
+49.211.83840
duesseldorf@hpp.com
www.hpp.com

The Düsseldorf-based practice HPP Architects is one of the few German architecture firms whose designs have shaped both reconstruction work after the Second World War, as well as architecture and urban development since the German reunification. The partnership was founded more than 80 years ago, and is now run by the fourth generation. It employs more than 360 staff at 10 sites, including Istanbul and Shanghai. Numerous HPP projects have shaped architectural history. These include the *Dreischeibenhaus* for the Thyssen group in Düsseldorf, as well as the EXPO Village in Shanghai, and the *AufSchalke* football stadium in Gelsenkirchen, Germany. The practice's range of services encompasses all architectural and general planning services; predominantly in projects involving administration and commercial buildings, hotels, hospitals, sporting and cultural establishments and urban construction and residential projects.

Photo: Christian Steinmetz

HWP Planungsgesellschaft mbH
Stuttgart

048

Okmeydani Training and Research Hospital

Istanbul, Turkey, 2019

The Okmeydani Training and Research Hospital in Istanbul is going to be the *hospital of the future*. Thanks to the interdisciplinary planning, led by HWP, not only does this hospital meet the very latest medicinal and technical requirements, but also sets new standards when it comes to sustainable building and the design of large earthquake-proof structures. Because Istanbul is in a region that is highly susceptible to earthquakes, a design according to static requirements was essential. Therefore Werner Sobek a civil engineer from Stuttgart developed an earthquake isolation system. The basis of this concept involves special pillars that are fitted with floor isolators, which are connected to a solid floor plate. The floor plate and the load-bearing walls are firmly affixed with floor studs. Due to that flexible design, the building's shell can react to movement, without collapsing in the event of an earthquake. The communication technology, especially the solid connection between the IT network to the clinic's medicinal technology, was also planned on the premise of a possible heavy earthquake occurring. Even after a seismographic catastrophe, the new hospital should be able to continue operations without interruption. The new complex of buildings allows rapid expansion of capacity if required. The buildings' surrounding areas, including green spaces, have been designed to be used as an immediate protection zone for civilians, and also serve as a space resource in case medicinal care facilities need to be erected temporarily.

SIGVARIS

048
Okmeydani Training and Research Hospital
Istanbul, Turkey, 2019

049
New-build Hospital Am Plattenwald
Bad Friedrichshall, Germany, 2016

Photo: Markus Bachmann

Photo: Peter Horn

050 Diagnostic-Internal-Neurological Centre, of the
Carl-Gustav-Carus University Hospital, of the Technical University Dresden
Dresden, Germany, 2012

Working together in interdisciplinary teams of architects, program managers, medical engineers, and laboratory engineers – that is our key to developing the best solutions for complex assignments.

051
Merck Serono S.A., Large Scale Biotech
Vevey, Switzerland, 2011

Photo: Thomas Jantscher

052
Institute of Nanotechnology at the Research Centre Karlsruhe
Karlsruhe, Germany, 2008

Photo: Klaus P. Müller

0.4
1.3
1.2

HWP Planungsgesellschaft mbH

The planning and realisation of complex medical research and care facilities, such as hospitals, university clinics, special clinics and rehabilitation clinics, forms the centre of competency of HWP Planungsgesellschaft, in Stuttgart. The company was founded in 1970 and has 140 employees today. There are seven other sites, including offices in Istanbul, Cairo and Tripoli. Beside their proven expertise in healthcare, the highly specialised planners and engineers are also able to demonstrate extensive experience in education, research and industrial sectors. Furthermore HWP Planungsgesellschaft is known as one of the first companies in that business sector to use Building Information Modelling (BIM). This innovative approach in planning unifies all available data relating to a construction project into one digital model. By contributing their own information, all stakeholders involved in the planning and realisation of the building project take part in the further development of this model. Every BIM model is sort of a project's *planning DNA* that contains the entire data relating to a building, which can then be used for analysis and operational purposes, as well as for further development.

Herbert Klein, Jason King, Frank Wachholz, Vanessa Jack (left to right)

Rotenbergstrasse 8
70190 Stuttgart – Germany
+49.711.1662-0
hwp@hwp-planung.de
www.hwp-planung.de

ISA Internationales Stadtbauatelier

Stuttgart

053

Development of the new city Lijiang

Lijiang, China, 2005

The development of the new Chinese city Lijiang demonstrates how the architects and urban developers were able to put these requirements into practice. The starting point for the development was the historical town of the same name, which lies 2,400 m above sea level, on the edge of the Himalayas. The planning area for the newly created town of Yulong, 6 km away, stretches between two mountains. The structures of the city of Lijiang, which came into being over the course of centuries, were projected into the development covering an area of 490 ha, and were used as the matrix for the new town. It is just as dense and compact as the historical example, but the modern buildings are commensurate with the expectations of 21st century architecture, both functionally and architecturally. Its diverse and varied façade designs reference the construction traditions that are typical of the region.

053

Development of the new city Lijiang

Lijiang, China, 2005

053

Development of the new city Lijiang

Lijiang, China, 2005

054

The council of representatives compound

Baghdad, Iraq, 2012

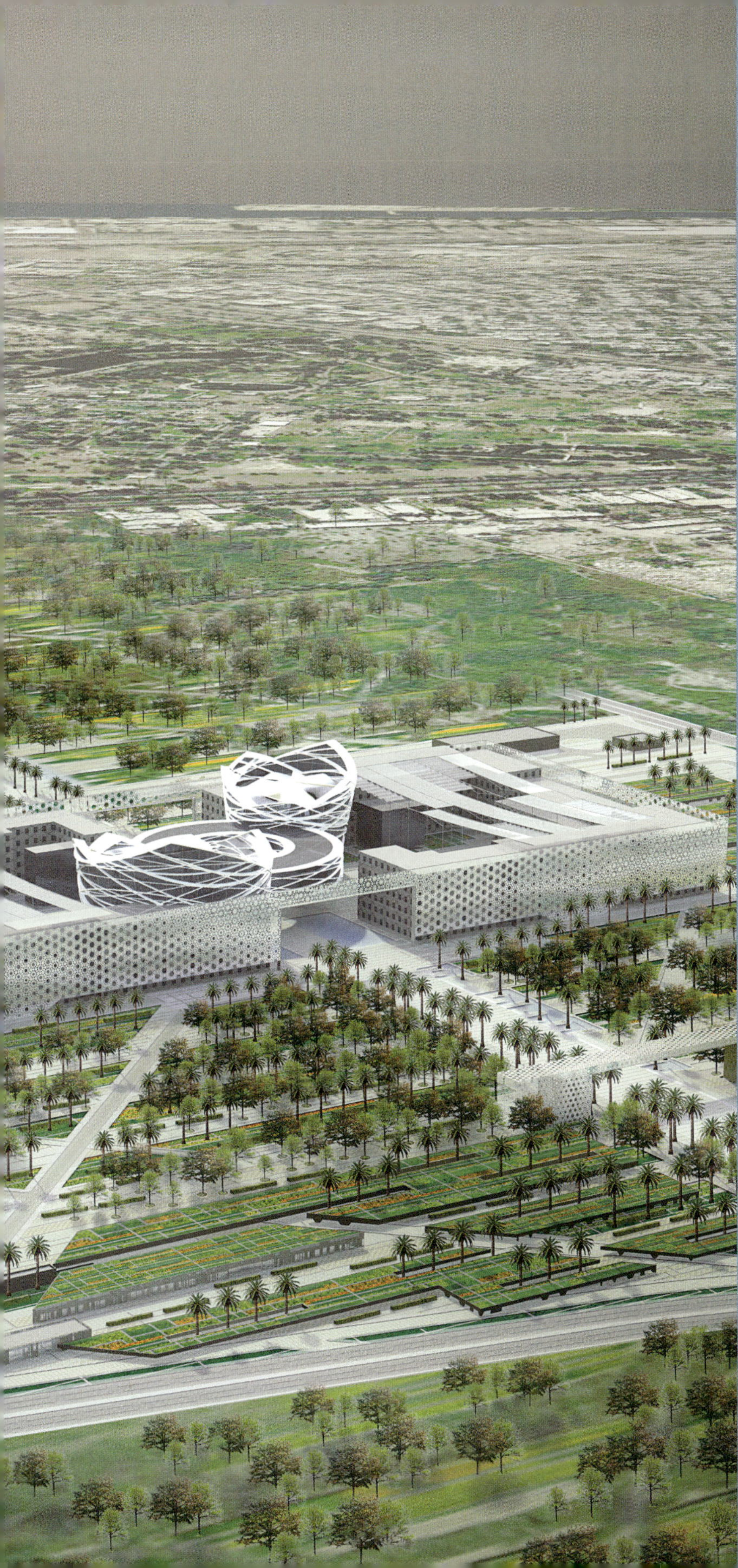

The City Image is not only the visual appearance of a city, but furthermore its complex entity of happenings and experiences, as well as the resulting – conscious and unconscious – emotions, attitudes and opinions.

055
Masterplan Taif
Taif, Saudi Arabia, 2014

056

Urban structure concept of Schmel

Dudelang, Luxemburg, 2009

ISA Internationales Stadtbauatelier
Furtbachstrasse 10
70178 Stuttgart – Germany
+49.711.6403031
contact@stadtbauatelier.de
www.stadtbauatelier.de

Anyone wanting to design and build entire towns or cities requires the experience of town planners, architects, landscape architects, geographers, traffic planners, and municipal economists. These are the conditions in which the Stuttgart-based ISA Internationales Stadtbauatelier, founded in 1978, operates. The company is active worldwide, and specialises in the design of complex socio-spatial contexts in which people and their needs are both starting points and guiding principles. In practice, this urban planning design ideal not only brings about an environment that fulfills the concrete material expectations of its inhabitants, but also takes their non-material, spiritual and sensual needs seriously.

K+P Architekten
Munich

057
Munich Airport Terminal 2 Satellite
Munich Airport, Germany, 2016

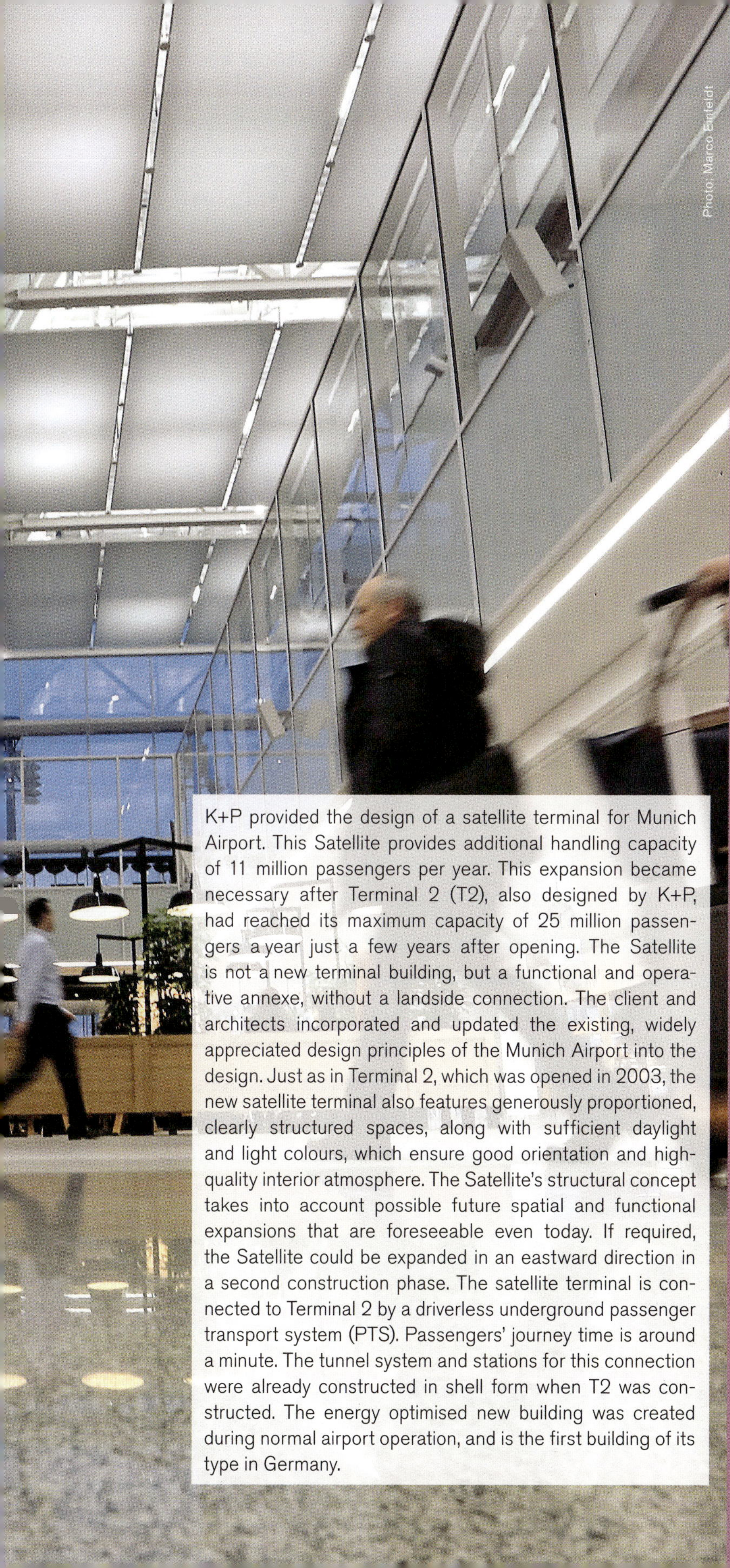

Photo: Marco Einfeldt

K+P provided the design of a satellite terminal for Munich Airport. This Satellite provides additional handling capacity of 11 million passengers per year. This expansion became necessary after Terminal 2 (T2), also designed by K+P, had reached its maximum capacity of 25 million passengers a year just a few years after opening. The Satellite is not a new terminal building, but a functional and operative annexe, without a landside connection. The client and architects incorporated and updated the existing, widely appreciated design principles of the Munich Airport into the design. Just as in Terminal 2, which was opened in 2003, the new satellite terminal also features generously proportioned, clearly structured spaces, along with sufficient daylight and light colours, which ensure good orientation and high-quality interior atmosphere. The Satellite's structural concept takes into account possible future spatial and functional expansions that are foreseeable even today. If required, the Satellite could be expanded in an eastward direction in a second construction phase. The satellite terminal is connected to Terminal 2 by a driverless underground passenger transport system (PTS). Passengers' journey time is around a minute. The tunnel system and stations for this connection were already constructed in shell form when T2 was constructed. The energy optimised new building was created during normal airport operation, and is the first building of its type in Germany.

058 Munich Airport Terminal 2
Main central hall with Munich Airport Center
Munich Airport, Germany, 2003

Photo: Stefan Müller-Naumann Fotodesign

Photo: Stefan Müller-Naumann/Fotodesign

059 Munich Airport Terminal 2
Canopy South on departure level 04
Munich Airport, Germany, 2003

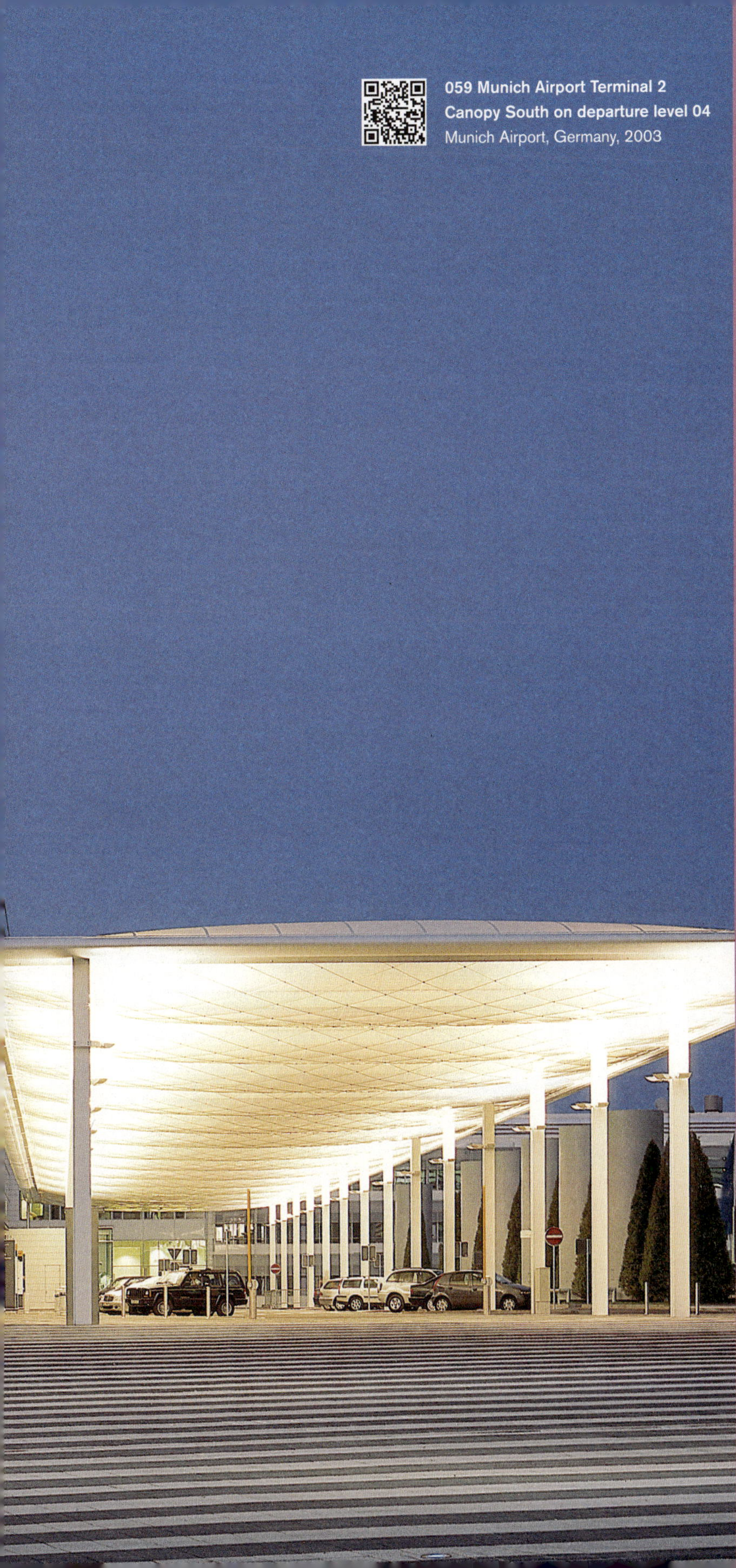

Photo: Christoph Stepan architecture photography

060

BMW Headquarters Munich

Frankfurter Ring, Germany, 2009

061

Major Refurbishment of the Boschetsrieder Siedlung

Munich, Germany, 2009

Photo: Sascha Kletzsch

Quality counts! We – architects and clients – should talk more about the quality of design, materials and spaces; because we stand for stability, durability and ultimately for cost effectiveness, in large and small scales, independently of situations, markets and cultures. Quality is noticeable!

062 Airport terminals for
Kigoma, Tabora, Shinyanga, Sumbawanga
Tanzania, 2016

Photo: vise.com

Managing Partners Jürgen Zschornack,
Norbert Koch, Wolfgang Voigt (from left)

Koch+Partner Architekten und Stadtplaner

The K+P Koch+Partner practice, based in Munich and Leipzig, is one of the few planning offices, which as well as having classic expertise in architecture and urban planning, also demonstrates international experience, acquired over many years, in designing airports. In this sector, complex approaches and urban planning expertise are just as in demand as custom, tailor-made solutions to highly specialised questions of detail. To this end, an interdisciplinary team comprising architects, urban and spatial planners, civil engineers, and interior architects are ready to supervise entire planning stages and project phases, as well as take on general planning work. Furthermore, K+P's portfolio also comprises competition management, energy consulting, as well as health and safety coordination.

Ismaninger Strasse 57
81675 Munich – Germany
+49.89.411880
www.kochundpartner.de
info@kochundpartner.de

KSP Jürgen Engel Architekten
Frankfurt am Main

The new construction of the National Library of China in Beijing emanated from the winning design by KSP Jürgen Engel Architekten as part of a competition. As a structure of national importance, it was expected to stand out from the everyday architecture in the Chinese capital. The self-assured, expansive gesture of the building, which does not reach into the sky – unlike most new buildings – but stretches out horizontally, is supported by a contemporary yet classically structured form of architecture: base, main hall, roof. Whilst the base area of Asia's largest library, with a total of 5 floors, houses the literary collection, comprising around 12 million books, the glazed hall with a foyer, cafeteria, and entrance to the reading room with 2000 seats is an area dedicated to the present and is spanned by a spectacular roof that projects far out at the sides. This earthquake-proof construction made of a 10 m-high steel framework and with a span of ca. 60 m is defined as a separate area and provides space for the digital collection over two levels.

063

National Library of China

Beijing, China, 2008

Photo: Hans Schlupp

063
National Library of China
Beijing, China, 2008

Photo: Hans Schlupp

Photo: Hans Schlupp

The architect's aim is to find a clear shape for complex inter-linkages. Our understanding of architecture is rooted in the present but shows great respect for architectural heritage. For every building task, irrespective of the size, we prefer to adopt a new approach for each building assignment depending on the location, context, and purpose and to provide a specific response to every architectural question.

063
National Library of China
Beijing, China, 2008

064

Meixi Urban Helix

Changsha, China, 2016

065

Science and Technology City

Qingdao, China, 2011

066
Tianjin Art Museum
Tianjin, China, 2012

Photo: Shuhe Photography

Jürgen Engel

Photo: Kirsten Bucher

KSP Jürgen Engel Architekten GmbH

With over 250 employees and offices in Berlin, Braunschweig, Frankfurt am Main, Munich, Hanoi, and Beijing, KSP Jürgen Engel Architekten is one of the biggest architectural offices in Germany. It made its international breakthrough with the winning design in the competition surrounding the construction of the new National Library of China, which was soon followed by other commissions in the Cathay region. The KSP Jürgen Engel Architekten portfolio ranges from solitary buildings for art and culture, to office and business premises, right through to hospitals, housing estates, and extensive urban developments. Besides classic design and planning services, the firm has its own specialised and experienced departments that also provide general planning and building management services, and is thus able to completely handle a project.

Hanauer Landstrasse 287-289
60314 Frankfurt am Main – Germany
+49.69.944394-0
info@ksp-architekten.de
www.ksp-architekten.de

LAVA Laboratory for Visionary Architecture Stuttgart

Visualisation: LAVA / moka studio

067

King Abdulaziz City of Science and Technology (KASCT)

Riyadh, Saudi Arabia, 2016

For the King Abdulaziz City of Science and Technology (KASCT), an innovative research campus in the Saudi Arabian capital Riyadh, the research building that came into being is not only the centre of the site, but equally a landmark in the capital that can be seen from afar. The 20-storey newbuild provides space for 1,700 staff, and conceptually, is strictly fitted to meet the specific cultural and climatic requirements of its location. Therefore, circulation and the building's technology were not placed in the core of the building, but instead integrated into the solidly constructed structures of the east and west façade. As a result, on the one hand, necessary protection against solar radiation was conceptionally incorporated into the architecture; and on the other hand, a generous and genuine spatial volume results in the building's interior. This interior features staggered levels that open out into the varied atriums, which alternatively face north and south. This ensures that lots of light enters the interior, which thanks to the luxuriant greenery, is transformed into an oasis.

068
The Square3
Berlin, Germany, 2012

Visualisation: LAVA / moka-studio

069

SIPCHEM PADC Laboratory

Al Khobar, Saudi Arabia, 2014

Photo: Trevor Hutley

Green is the new black: LAVA aspires to form the architecture of tomorrow characterised by a low environmental impact but a high architectural and sculptural quality.

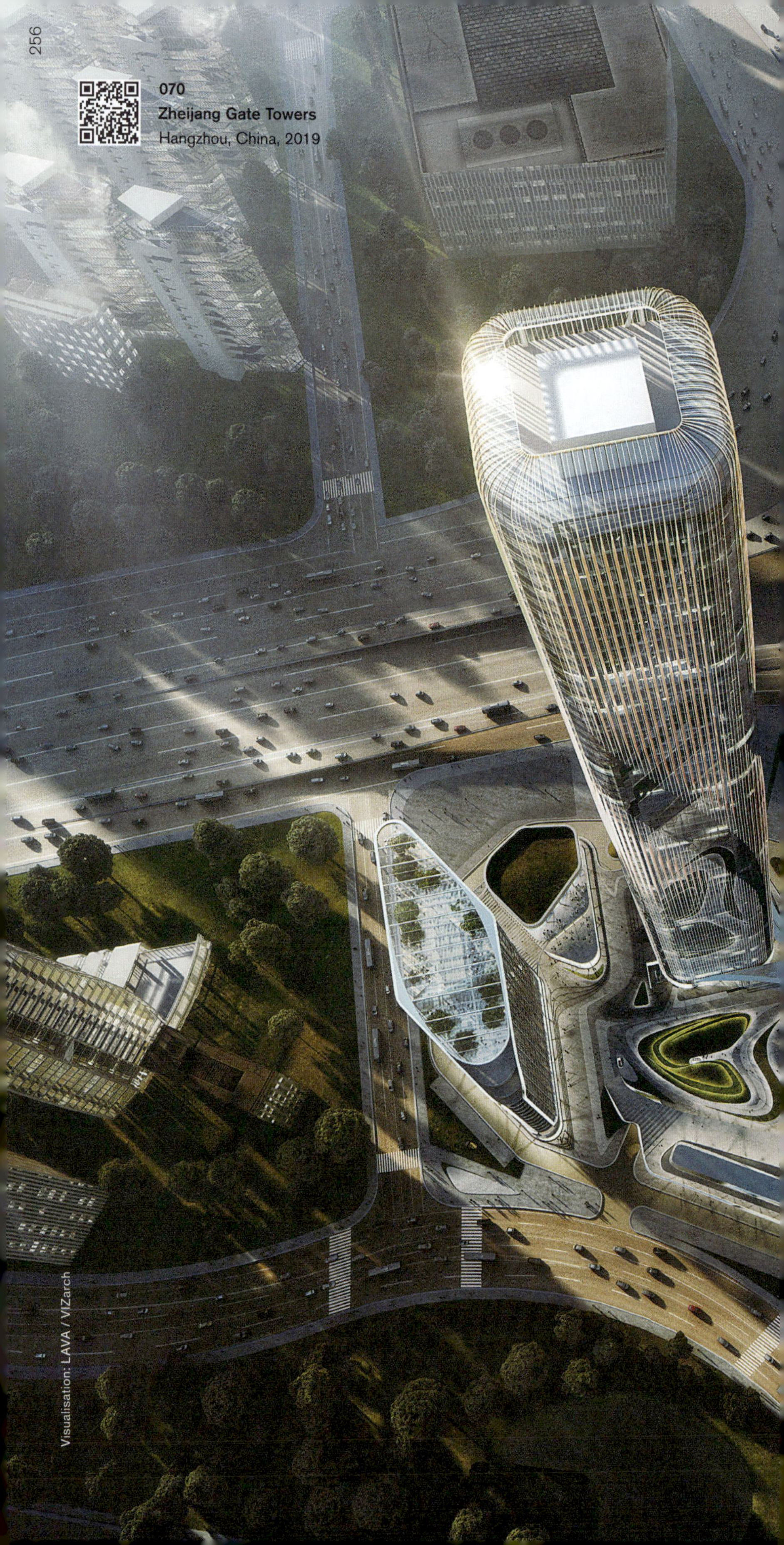

070
Zheijang Gate Towers
Hangzhou, China, 2019

Visualisation: LAVA / VIZarch

071
Masdar City Centre
Abu Dhabi, UAE, 2009

Visualisation: LAVA / MIR

Photo: Jonathan Andrew

072
Philips Lighting Headquarters
Eindhoven, Netherlands, 2015

LAVA Laboratory for Visionary Architecture

LAVA is an international network of specialists that works on visionary architectural and urban planning projects across the entire world. The company, founded in 2007, employs around 50 staff at its offices in Berlin, Stuttgart, and Sydney, and takes its inspiration from nature, technology and human ingenuity. In their designs, the architects strive for an integration of space, structure and adornment. From the conceptual and visualisation stages, right up to the creation of model-like prototypes, LAVA works with the very latest digital design tools. The list of projects they have realised spans hotels, office complexes, high rises, museums, sport stadiums, residential and commercial buildings, plus resorts in Germany, Australia, Mexico, China and the Near East.

Laboratory Stuttgart
Wolframstrasse 20b
70191 Stuttgart – Germany
+4.711.72232901

Laboratory Berlin
Saarbrücker Strasse 24
10405 Berlin – Germany
+49.30.473747180

directors@l-a-v-a.net
www.l-a-v-a.net

Photo: Peter Bennetts

Meuser Architekten GmbH
Berlin

Photo: Alexei Naroditsky

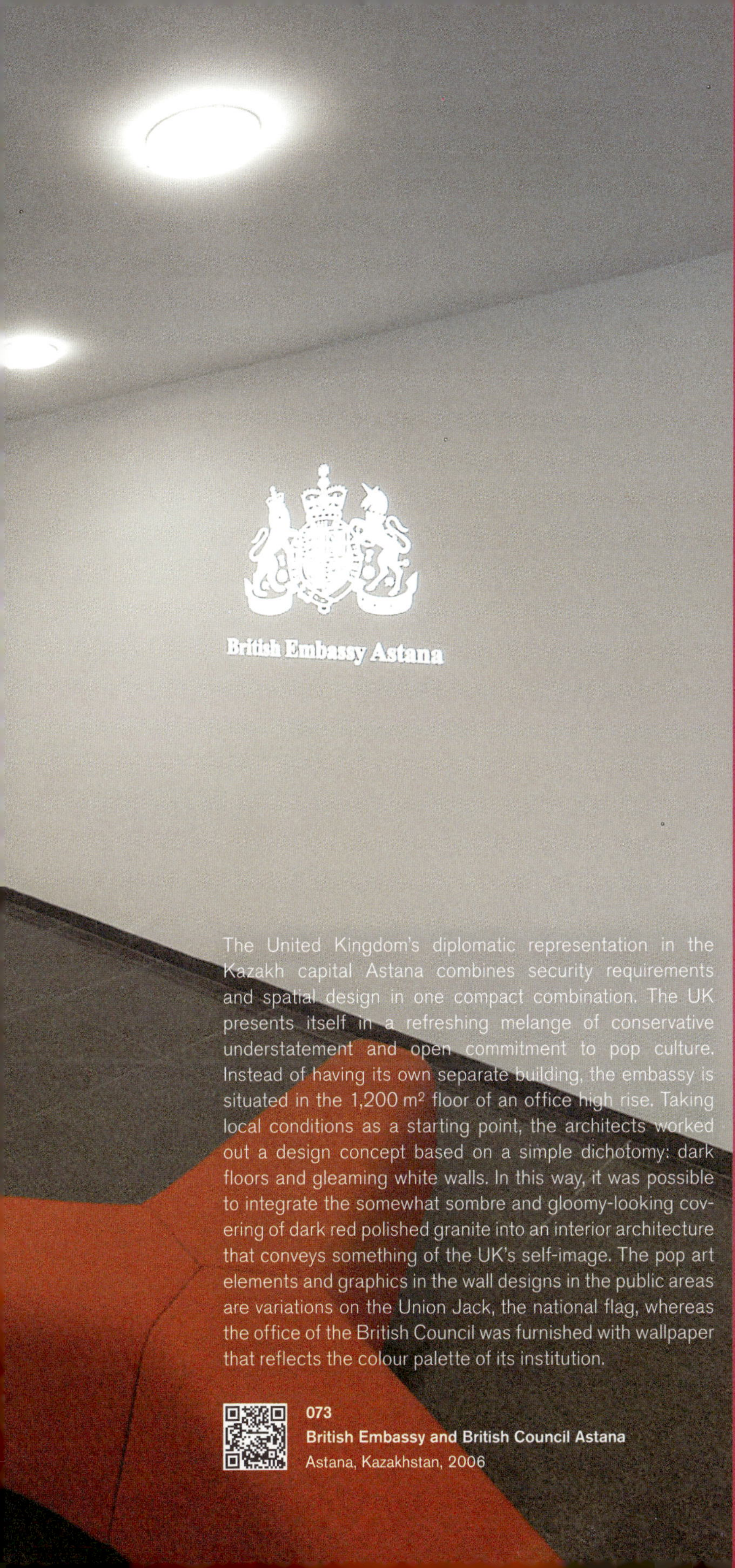

The United Kingdom's diplomatic representation in the Kazakh capital Astana combines security requirements and spatial design in one compact combination. The UK presents itself in a refreshing melange of conservative understatement and open commitment to pop culture. Instead of having its own separate building, the embassy is situated in the 1,200 m² floor of an office high rise. Taking local conditions as a starting point, the architects worked out a design concept based on a simple dichotomy: dark floors and gleaming white walls. In this way, it was possible to integrate the somewhat sombre and gloomy-looking covering of dark red polished granite into an interior architecture that conveys something of the UK's self-image. The pop art elements and graphics in the wall designs in the public areas are variations on the Union Jack, the national flag, whereas the office of the British Council was furnished with wallpaper that reflects the colour palette of its institution.

073
British Embassy and British Council Astana
Astana, Kazakhstan, 2006

074
Quiet Room, United Nations Headquarters
New York City, USA, 2013

075
Consulat General de France Almaty
Almaty, Kazakhstan, 2009

Rendering: Fabio Schilacci

We measure ourselves by our ability to make invaluable contributions to contemporary architecture and to promote a current architectural discourse. We believe that to think and build modern is to acknowledge the achievements of architectural history, learning from its mistakes in preparation for the future.

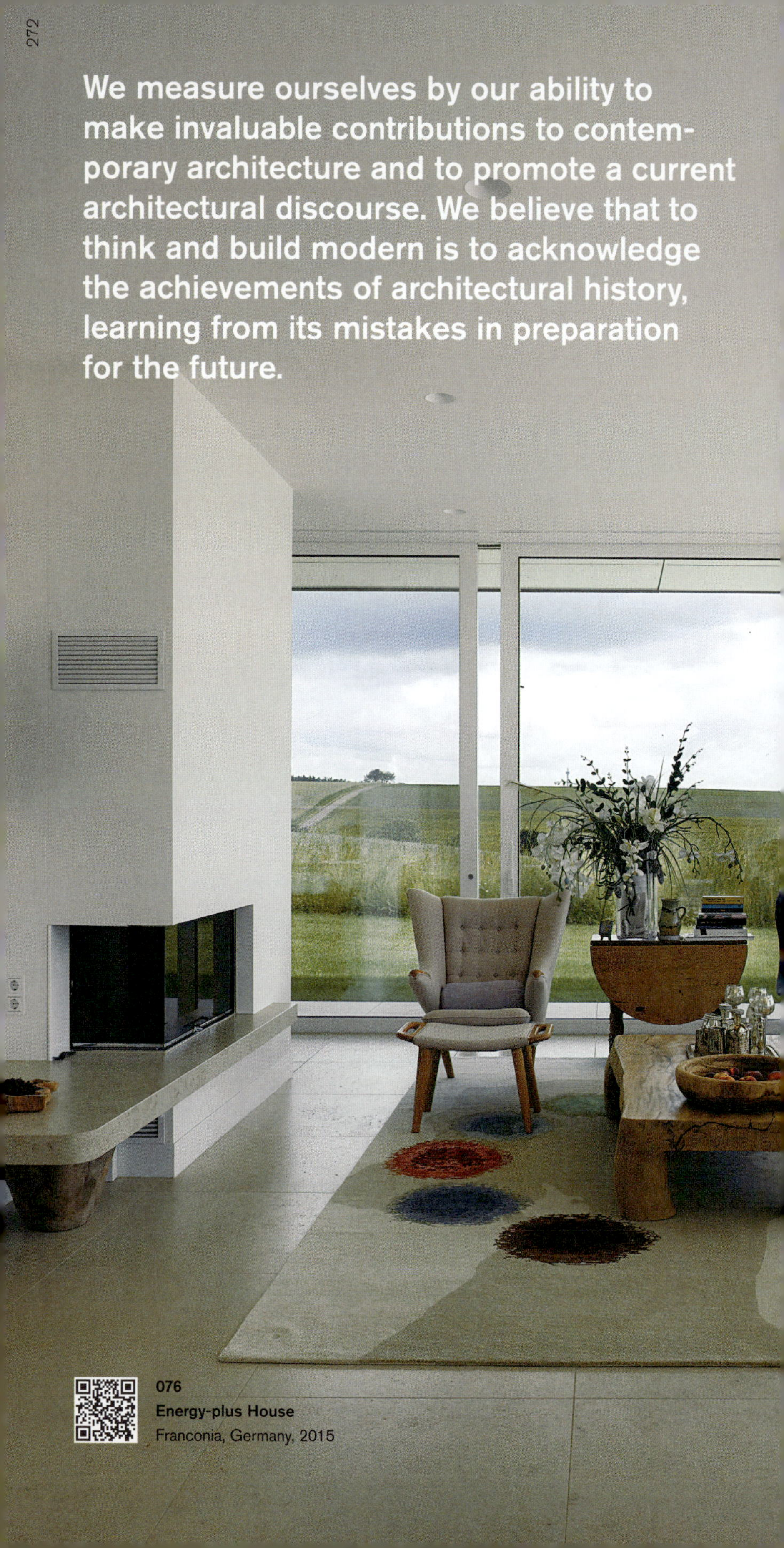

076
Energy-plus House
Franconia, Germany, 2015

Photo: Roland Halbe

Rendering: Andrei Mikhalenko

077
German Embassy Bamako
Bamako, Mali, 2018

078
German Embassy Ashgabat
Ashgabat, Turkmenistan, 2018

Rendering: Merdan Mamedov

Photo: Christoph Gößmann

Natascha and Philipp Meuser

Meuser Architekten GmbH

Since 1996, Meuser Architekten have been working in an interdisciplinary fashion as a team of planners, designers and editors on the interface of constructional practice and theory. Wherever in the world the practice has been active, their work bears witness to an intensive involvement with the location, its history and the respective conditions under which architecture develops. In doing so, their designs and implementation can be measured against the requirement to use people as the benchmark, and to respect that which is already in place. The practice can demonstrate numerous international projects in which their experience of working with listed buildings and ensuring that buildings are accessible to disabled users was as sought after as their special expertise in questions of safety and security.

Caroline-von-Humboldt-Weg 20
10117 Berlin – Germany
+49.30.20696920
info@meuser-architekten.de
www.meuser-architekten.de

Nattler Architekten

Essen

079
Hotel Franz
Essen, Germany, 2012

The integrative conference and city hotel Franz**** in Essen is a building that is equally welcoming to people with or without disabilities. This newbuild, which has complete disability access, comprises two separate wings, and houses the hotel operation, a convention centre and large kitchen. It is situated within the grounds of a charitable organisation. The ensemble of buildings enriches the sparsely developed area where it is situated with an inviting front side facing towards the urban space, and has a high recognition factor. The slightly set back, raised building with a Trespa® façade in warm wood colours modestly submits to the park-like environment, into which the room-high window fronts open. The 48 rooms of the hotel, along with all public areas, such as the conference and restaurant areas, are all fitted out so that people who are blind, deaf or who use wheelchairs are all able to orientate themselves and move around without help.

Photo: Michael Rasche

079
Hotel Franz
Essen, Germany, 2012

Our primary motivation is to come as close as possible to our clients' wishes and express them in a unique architectural form.

Photo: Michael Rasche

079

Hotel Franz

Essen, Germany, 2012

Photo: Franz Sales Haus

080
Media Markt
Dortmund, Germany, 2017

© avpgroup

081

Nordfeld

Bonn, Germany, 2019

© avpgroup

082
Sparkasse
Singen, Germany, 2017

© virtuell format

Nattler Architekten

Girardetstrasse 3-5
45131 Essen – Germany
+49.201.79981
info@nattlerarchitekten.de
www.nattlerarchitekten.de

The practice Nattler Architekten, founded in 1949 and based in Essen, can demonstrate a comprehensive experience in virtually all branches of architecture and construction planning. As well as architects and engineers, the permanent team, comprising around 40 members, also consists of staff specialising in all tasks that are part of the construction process, such as planners, and commercial and administrative experts. The wide variety of projects undertaken not only reflects these international developers' wide spectrum, but also the creative flair involved in the respective designs. Whether administration buildings or cultural institutions, commercial architecture or residential buildings – for every type of project, Nattler Architekten seek out a distinct, architecturally unique solution.

Heinz Hecht (left) and Heinz Nattler (right)

Nickl & Partner Architekten AG

Munich

083
Helmholtz Institute of the University of Ulm (HIU)
Ulm, Germany, 2014

The University of Ulm's Helmholtz Institute is situated in the science park in Obere Eselsberg, a new site for scientific organisations in the north of the city. The foundation for planning the new building was an existing masterplan, according to which the area would be developed step by step, to be developed into a modern centre for research. The Helmholtz centre, with its scientific focus on electrochemical energy storage, is a three-storey building that houses research and laboratory facilities. It provides a high degree of flexibility of space, and uses the modular principle. The outer and inner courtyard façades on the western side contain large rooms which, if required, can be divided into several laboratories, and so can easily be adapted to the requirements of the respective working environment. The various specialised laboratories are housed in the ground and lower levels, with office space situated above. Central communication areas enable encounters and interaction. The open inner courtyard is accessible from the ground floor, and enables a view of the seminar and meeting rooms, which are arranged towards the courtyard side. Thanks to the different sized holes punched into the distinctive perforated plate façade, a visual light show ensues, which bestows the building with its own quite unique relevance.

Photo: Werner Huthmacher

083
Helmholtz Institute of the University of Ulm (HIU)
Ulm, Germany, 2014

084
University Hospital Frankfurt of the Goethe University
Frankfurt am Main, Germany, 2014

Photos: Werner Huthmacher

We are respectful of both – people and resources. We design architecture for tomorrow – and create built environments with added value. We find inspiration in bringing intelligent design to life.

084

University Hospital Frankfurt of the Goethe University

Frankfurt am Main, Germany, 2014

Photo: Werner Huthmacher

085

Institute of Structural Biology IBS

Grenoble, France, 2013

Photo: Ivan Lukasevic

086

Mother-Child and Surgical Centre, SZX Kaiser-Franz-Josef-Hospital

Vienna, Austria, 2016

Photo: Werner Huthmacher

086

Mother-Child and Surgical Centre, SZX Kaiser-Franz-Josef-Hospital

Vienna, Austria, 2016

Photo: Werner Huthmacher

Nickl & Partner Architekten AG

Office Munich
Lindberghstrasse 19
80939 Munich – Germany
+49.89.360514-0
mail@nickl-architekten.de

Office Berlin
Wikingerufer 7
10555 Berlin – Germany
+49.30.20051408-0
mail@nickl-architekten-berlin.de

Office Zurich
Hardstrasse 235
8005 Zurich – Switzerland
+41.43.5442750

Office Beijing
A709 SanLitun Soho,
Chaoyang District
100027 Beijing – China
mail@nickl-partner.cn

www.nickl-partner.com

The work of Nickl & Partner Architekten AG is distinguished by the constant search for the new, along with consistent quality in planning and realisation. Since being founded in 1979, the architectural practice with offices in Munich, Berlin, Zurich and Beijing has been able to accumulate excellent specialist knowledge, and has established itself as one of Germany's leading planning offices, specialising in healthcare, research and residential buildings. The conflict between highly complex construction projects requiring a high degree of functionality and rationality, and the more human elements, on the other hand, constantly leads the architects to innovative solutions, which combine the requirements for beauty and sustainability with technical and structural precision. The practice's high quality demands go hand in hand with the unity of academic theory and practice. Professor Christine Nickl-Weller holds lectures and conducts research at the Technical University of Berlin. Professor Hans Nickl lectures in Erfurt and is visiting professor at the Technical University of Berlin. Nickl & Partner Architekten AG is increasingly active internationally. The Munich-based architects have long since made a name for themselves with their projects in the rest of Europe, in the Arab states and Asia.

Photo: Holger Talinski

OBERMEYER

Munich

Since March 2014, a cosmopolitan clinic campus is being constructed in the oasis city of Al Ain, near Abu Dhabi, according to OBERMEYER's design. The architectural concept is based on the theme of a *healing oasis.* With approximately 700 beds, the hospital meets the most modern medical and building services demands, while at the same time takes the cultural and climatic conditions into account. In order to realise this large-scale project, within the approximately 38-month timescale, OBERMEYER's planners took advantage of BIM (Building Information Modelling) and the integration of the individual trades into one central three-dimensional model. Basic prerequisites for realising a planning volume of this size in an interdisciplinary way are not only special knowhow in relation to planning health facilities and medical equipment, but also well-functioning internal communication.

087
Al Ain Hospital
Abu Dhabi, United Arab Emirates, 2018

087
Al Ain Hospital
Abu Dhabi, United Arab Emirates, 2018

088
Jizdecka Theatre
Pilsen, Czech Republic, 2014

089

Campus Bayernoil Ingolstadt

Neustadt an der Donau, Germany, 2008

Photo: Michael Heinrich

We develop all projects jointly with our clients. In doing so, we elaborate architecturally and technically sophisticated solutions. Our teams have an interdisciplinary orientation, enabling us to design not only the building, but also its integration into the surrounding environment. To this end we prepare our projects to a high technological standard using Building Information Modeling (BIM).

090
German Embassy Tashkent
Tashkent, Uzbekistan, 2016

091

North Railway Station

Guangzhou, China, 2016 (Competition)

OBERMEYER
Planen + Beraten GmbH

Hansastrasse 40
80686 Munich – Germany
+49.89.5799-0
info@opb.de
www.opb.de

With more than 1,200 employees and numerous branch offices in Germany and abroad, the OBERMEYER Corporate Group, founded in Munich in 1958, is one of the largest independent consultancies in Germany. The interdisciplinary team of architects, engineers, landscape architects, and urban planners handles highly complex planning and building projects spanning architecture, urban and regional planning, as well as underground engineering and infrastructure projects all over the world. With various in-house specialist departments, OBERMEYER does not just offer planning services for individual disciplines, but complete planning extending from the first study right up to completion, and all from one source. In doing so, the planners' solutions not only meet requirements for functionality and economic efficiency, but also take special account of sustainability and energy efficiency aspects. The designs are implemented using the very latest technical methods, such as BIM and GIS.

ORANGE BLU building solutions
Stuttgart

One of the practice's countless international projects is the new construction of the British embassy in the Georgian capital Tbilisi. The strictly cubist ensemble, situated at the foot of a hill in the south of the city, comprises the representation, consular section and the ambassador's residence. The terraced complex's hillside location offers a clear view over Tbilisi and the landscape of the Caucasus – a privilege afforded the architecture due to its deploying local materials and building traditions. In order to integrate all the functions of a modern diplomatic mission into one shared location, the residence – the home of the ambassador – was included as part of the actual embassy buildings. While the drawn-out transoms of the embassy and visa department feature a frontage made from basalt, as is locally typical, the residence, which sits enthroned above all else, was enveloped in a gleaming metal body, whose patterns are reminiscent of those of traditional Georgian woodcut art.

Photo: Dennis Gilbert/VIEW

092
British Embassy Tbilisi
Tbilisi, Georgia, 2010

092
British Embassy Tbilisi
Tbilisi, Georgia, 2010

Photo: Dennis Gilbert/VIEW

092
British Embassy Tbilisi
Tbilisi, Georgia, 2010

Photo: Dennis Gilbert/VIEW

093
Library and Academy at the Peace Palace
Den Haag, Netherlands, 2007

Photo: Peter de Ruig

We enjoy engaging in tasks that may initially seem impossible: complex buildings, difficult construction requirements and challenging urban planning scenarios to be resolved in high quality architecture worldwide.

Photo: Peter de Ruig

094
Visitor Center at the Peace Palace
Den Haag, Netherlands, 2012

094
Visitor Center at the Peace Palace
Den Haag, Netherlands, 2012

Photo: Peter de Ruig

Audio Tour
Welcome
Bienvenue
War and Peace
Guerre et Paix
Dulce bellum
inexpertis
Le Palais de la Paix
The Peace Palace
Het Vredespaleis

ORANGE BLU building solutions

Whoever understands how to combine modern architecture with its historical roots, and who is able to create distinct, contemporary architecture on that basis, is a worthy heir to James Stirling, winner of the Pritzker Prize. The Stuttgart-based practice, formed from a merger of the Wilford Schupp and zsp practices, regards itself as being bound to his legacy. The founders now combine all the experience that they gained in large international practices into one joint undertaking, which with its nearly 35 employees is set to face the challenges of an international market. In its plans, the team succeeds in creating identity-forging architecture from a synthesis of architectural traditions and technological advances. The practice's transparent process management utilises digital planning models (BIM) and a pronounced culture of communication between all stakeholders.

Seyfferstrasse 34
70197 Stuttgart – Germany
+49.711.669830
mail@orangeblu.com
www.orangeblu.com

[phase **eins**].
Berlin

4

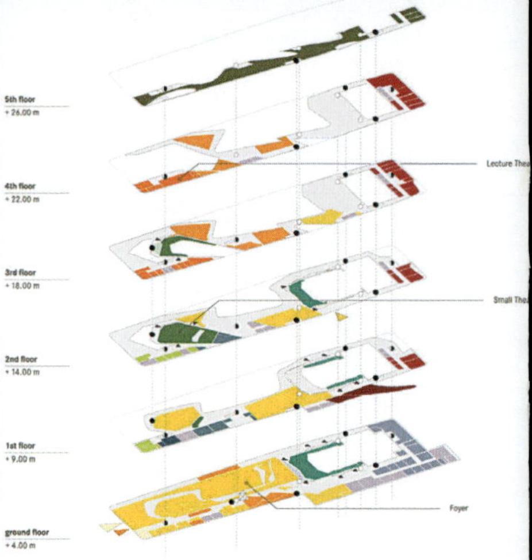
5th floor
+ 26.00 m
4th floor
+ 22.00 m
3rd floor
+ 18.00 m
2nd floor
+ 14.00 m
1st floor
+ 9.00 m
ground floor
+ 4.00 m
Lecture Thea
Small Thea
Foyer

Urban Landing
New road access

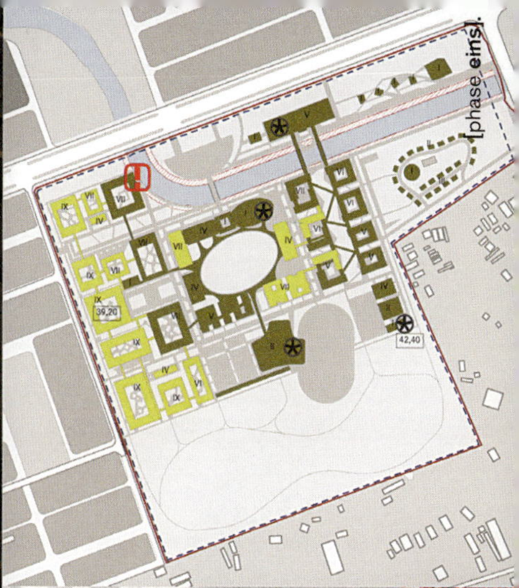
39,20
42,40

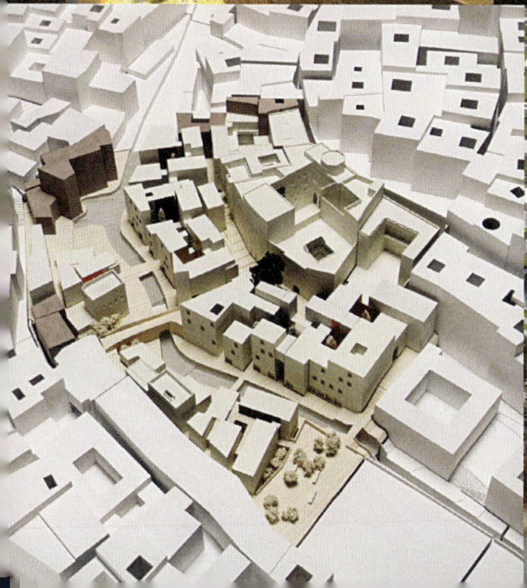

BMW GROUP
FIZ FUTURE
AUSLOBUNG
BERICHT

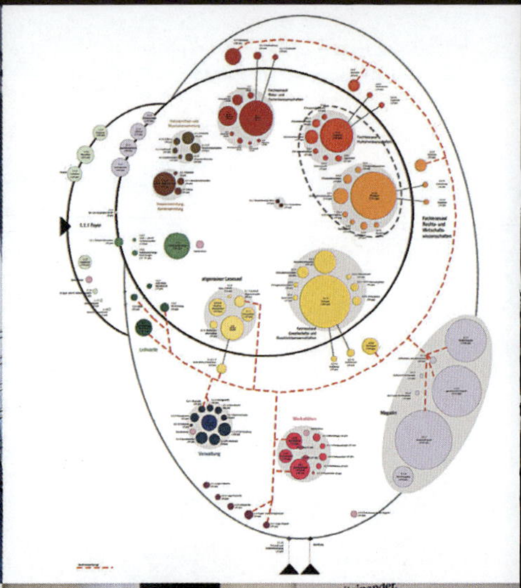

15.4w
15.4v
IBG-3
Lysimeter
15.5u
15.7u
15.8u
15.22u
West-Ring
IBG-1
IBG-3
ICS-4
15.15
15.19
14.4
14.2u
W17
14.6w

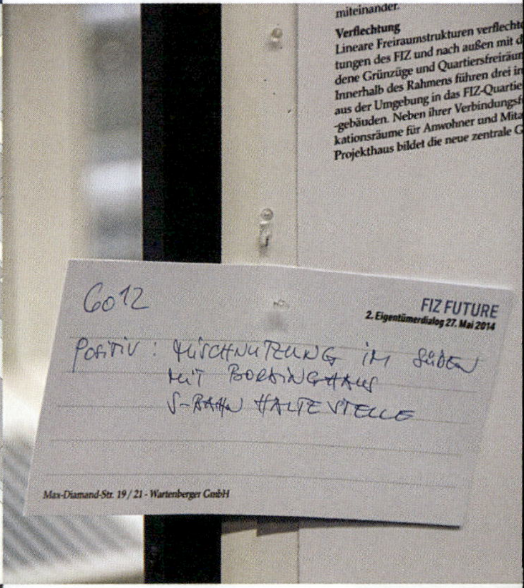
miteinander.
Verflechtung
6012
FIZ FUTURE
2. Eigentümerdialog 27. Mai 2014
POSITIV: MISCHNUTZUNG IM SÜDEN
MIT BOARDINGHAUS
S-BAHN HALTESTELLE
Max-Diamand-Str. 19 / 21 - Wartenberger GmbH

Prof. Dr. Elisabeth Merk

6. Area and volume calculations
7a. Explanatory report on urban design and architecture
suitable for publication.

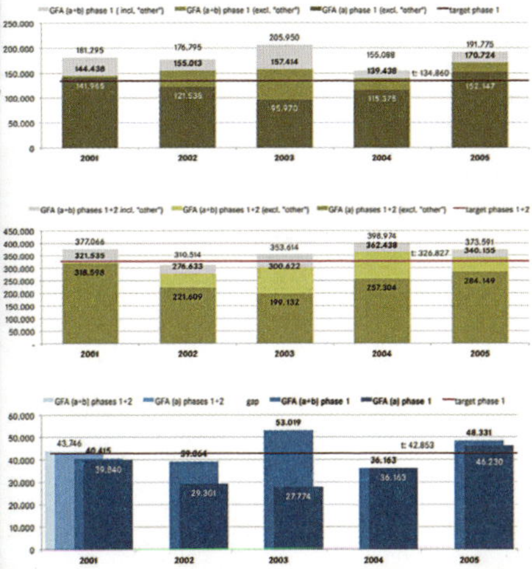
GFA (a+b) phase 1 (incl. "other")
GFA (a+b) phase 1 (excl. "other")
GFA (a) phase 1 (excl. "other")
target phase 1
250.000
200.000
150.000
100.000
50.000
0
181.295
144.438
141.965
176.795
155.013
121.536
205.950
157.414
95.970
155.088
139.438
115.375
t: 134.860
191.775
170.724
152.147
2001
2002
2003
2004
2005
GFA (a+b) phases 1+2 incl. "other")
GFA (a+b) phases 1+2 (excl. "other")
GFA (a) phases 1+2 (excl. "other")
target phases 1+2
450.000
400.000
350.000
300.000
250.000
200.000
150.000
100.000
50.000
377.066
321.535
318.598
310.514
276.633
221.609
353.614
300.622
199.132
398.974
362.438
257.304
t: 326.827
373.591
340.155
284.149
2001
2002
2003
2004
2005
GFA (a+b) phases 1+2
GFA (a) phases 1+2
gap
GFA (a+b) phase 1
GFA (a) phase 1
target phase 1
60.000
50.000
40.000
30.000
20.000
10.000
0
43.746
40.415
39.840
39.064
29.301
53.019
27.774
36.163
36.163
t: 42.853
48.331
46.230
2001
2002
2003
2004
2005

Übersicht

Jury meetings and colloquia

9. Mai 2014
FIZ FUTURE
SITZUNG DES PREISGERICH
ZWEISTUFIGER PLANUNGSWETTBEWERB
IN MÜNCHEN

Jury discussion

International open project competition – Place Lalla Yeddouna in the Medina of Fez, Morocco

Jury discussion

Jabal Khandama Development Project, Makkah Al-Mukaramah, Kingdom of Saudi Arabia

Jury discussion

Art competition – Staatsoper Unter den Linden, Berlin, Germany

Benjamin Hossbach

Christian Lehmhaus

[phase **eins**].

Project consultants + design competition organizers

[phase eins]. is an architectural practice founded in 1998 in Berlin with an unusual focus. The architects working here neither design buildings, nor spend time on construction sites; instead, they exclusively supervise projects during the initial stage of projects, the *phase eins*. The company provides assistance with the strategic orientation of a project, clarification of site conditions, and organization of the selection of the most suitable design and designer for the project. Together all these services define the core activities at [phase eins]., the management of design competitions, for which [phase eins]. has earned its worldwide reputation. The practice can look back on more than 100 successfully completed projects in Europe, Africa, the Americas, and Asia, including urban development master plans, administration buildings for businesses and governments, cultural buildings, universities, and research institutions. Competition management requires not only expertise in planning and more technical areas, but also relevant experience in dealing with authorities and knowledge of applicable legal conditions. Since large, complex projects rely on the communication between developers, planners, and the respective authorities, mutual trust is the basis of cooperation. The practice therefore creates the foundations with an individually tailored process management plan. This is the only way to combine the interests of developers with the very highest architectural standards, whilst ensuring that the project's realisation is both as economical and creative as possible. In other words: This is the only way to achieve building culture.

Cuxhavener Strasse 12-13
10555 Berlin – Germany
+49.30.315931-0
office@phase1.de
www.phase1.de

Rainer Schmidt
Landschaftsarchitekten Munich

095

Munich Airport Parking Level

Munich, Germany, 2003

From a planning point of view, the conversion of the Munich Airport's two terminal buildings from the *airport in the countryside* into a functional *airport region* complex was a success. As an ensemble, the stopover areas, passageways, and outdoor space form an unified image, which turns what was purely a transition point into a place of sojourn, meetings and communication. The open space was also designed according to the same principle. Starting with the existing building structures as a base, Rainer Schmidt Landscape Architects and Urban Planners have developed a concept that, with the materials selected, the spatial setting, and the technical nature of the site, has come to reflect the surrounding Bavarian scenery. Since the airport commenced operations in 2003, the 12 ha site has also become a point of attraction for the inhabitants of the region. They take advantage of the urban structures that have come into being here, such as the restaurants, cafes and shops, just as if it were a completely normal town.

Photo: Stefan Müller-Naumann

096
Park Killesberg
Stuttgart, Germany, 2012

Photo: Raffaella Sirtoli

097
Central Park - Parkstadt Schwabing
Munich, Germany, 2002

Photo: Raffaella Sirtoli

098
Culture Wave City
Hangzhou, China, 2009

© OBERMEYER Planen+Beraten

Origin is ever-present. It is not a beginning, because the beginning is bound to the notion of time; and the present is not merely now, today, nor a moment. It is not a part of time, but a holistic achievement.

Jean Gebser: Origine et Présent

099
Doha Aerospace City
Doha, Qatar, 2010

© RSLA, KPF Architects

100
Multifunctional Medical Center
St. Petersburg, Russia, 2014

© RSLA, Nickl & Partner Architekten

Rainer Schmidt Landschaftsarchitekten

For more than a quarter of a century, Rainer Schmidt Landscape Architects and Urban Planners have been planning and realising large projects under the framework of public and infrastructural building projects, including projects in North Africa, as well as in the Middle and Far East. The practice maintains its main office in Munich and two other branches in Berlin and Bernburg, Germany. The aim of the 30-person team is to inject some contemporary feeling into the relationship between nature and culture, space and society. The urban development masterplans and landscape interventions bear witness to a harmonic relationship between creativity and function, and always take into consideration their effect on the quality of space for people and nature.

Office Munich
Von-der-Tann-Strasse 7
80539 Munich – Germany
+49.89.2025350

Office Berlin
Reichenberger Strasse 113a
10999 Berlin – Germany
+49.30.7890780

Office Bernburg
Friedrichstrasse 17
06406 Bernburg – Germany
+49.3471.628178

info@rainerschmidt.com
www.rainerschmidt.com

hoto: Raffaela Sirtoli

RhineScheme GmbH
Eiterfeld

101

Cultural Centre Tianjin

Tianjin, China, 2012

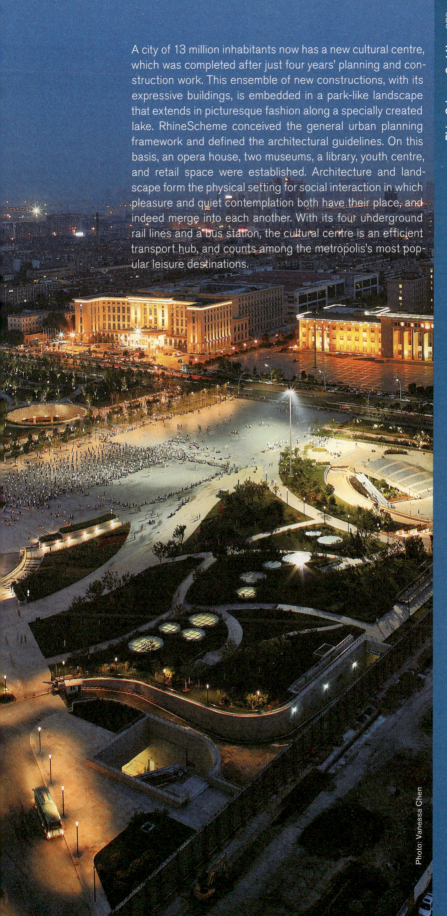

A city of 13 million inhabitants now has a new cultural centre, which was completed after just four years' planning and construction work. This ensemble of new constructions, with its expressive buildings, is embedded in a park-like landscape that extends in picturesque fashion along a specially created lake. RhineScheme conceived the general urban planning framework and defined the architectural guidelines. On this basis, an opera house, two museums, a library, youth centre, and retail space were established. Architecture and landscape form the physical setting for social interaction in which pleasure and quiet contemplation both have their place, and indeed merge into each other. With its four underground rail lines and a bus station, the cultural centre is an efficient transport hub, and counts among the metropolis's most popular leisure destinations.

Photo: Vanessa Chen

101

Cultural Centre Tianjin

Tianjin, China, 2012

Photo: Christian Gahl

Photo: Christian Gahl

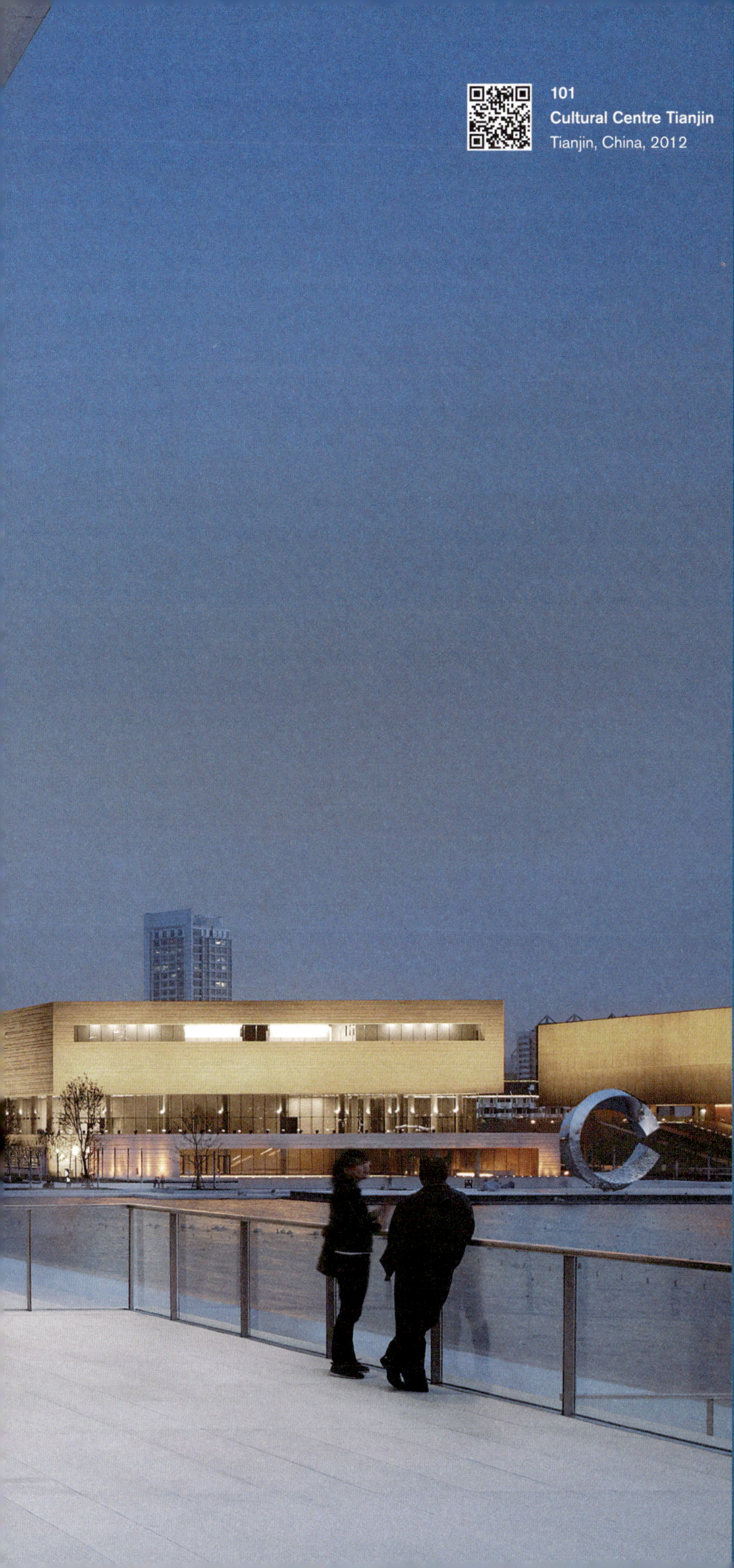

101
Cultural Centre Tianjin
Tianjin, China, 2012

102
XiXi Wetland Park Exhibition Centre
Hangzhou, China, 2014

Photo: JF Photography

103

Smart City & Eco City

Wuhan, China, 2013

104

Intellectual Property Publishing House

Beijing, China, 2016

Photo: studio SHUHE

RhineScheme GmbH

Even with the choice of its name, the RhineScheme practice leaves no doubt as to its origins and self-image. The Rhine therefore serves as a joint home that connects all nine associated partners, even overcoming national borders in its importance as an identity-forging European symbol. At the same time, it is a symbol of the free-flowing ideas that design processes have been feeding on from time immemorial. With nearly 100 employees in its branches in Cologne, Frankfurt am Main, Leipzig, Beijing, and Philadelphia, the practice can draw upon more than 40 years' experience in all relevant planning disciplines. RhineScheme has realised countless worldwide projects spanning urban planning, architecture, interior architecture as well as landscape design. It has acquired an excellent reputation for extremely complex projects, especially in China.

Office Eiterfeld
Am Hirzacker 5
36132 Eiterfeld – Germany
+49.6672.868470
info@rhinescheme.com

Office Cologne
Agrippinawerft 18
50678 Cologne – Germany
+49.221.9216430
cologne@rhinescheme.com

Office Beijing
3, Dong Binhe Lu 2-2-401
100013 Beijing – China
+86.10.84221360
beijing@rhinescheme.com

www.rhinescheme.com

RSAA Sustainable Architecture
and Urban Design Cologne

105

Jining City Culture Center

Jining City, China, 2017

The Jining City Culture Center is a new urban quarter, south of the historical city of Jining, the birthplace of Confucius, in the eastern Chinese province of Shandong. On a site spanning nearly 53 ha, the west of the new city features a cultural centre including museums, a library and a centre for folk art. The aim of RSAA's urban development masterplan is to bring the cultural buildings already in existence into a more harmonious context and to connect them with the predominantly business-orientated district in the east of the city via outdoor facilities. It also succeeds in winning the Taibai lake as a part of new city by means of providing a visual bond.

105
Jining City Culture Center
Jining City, China, 2017

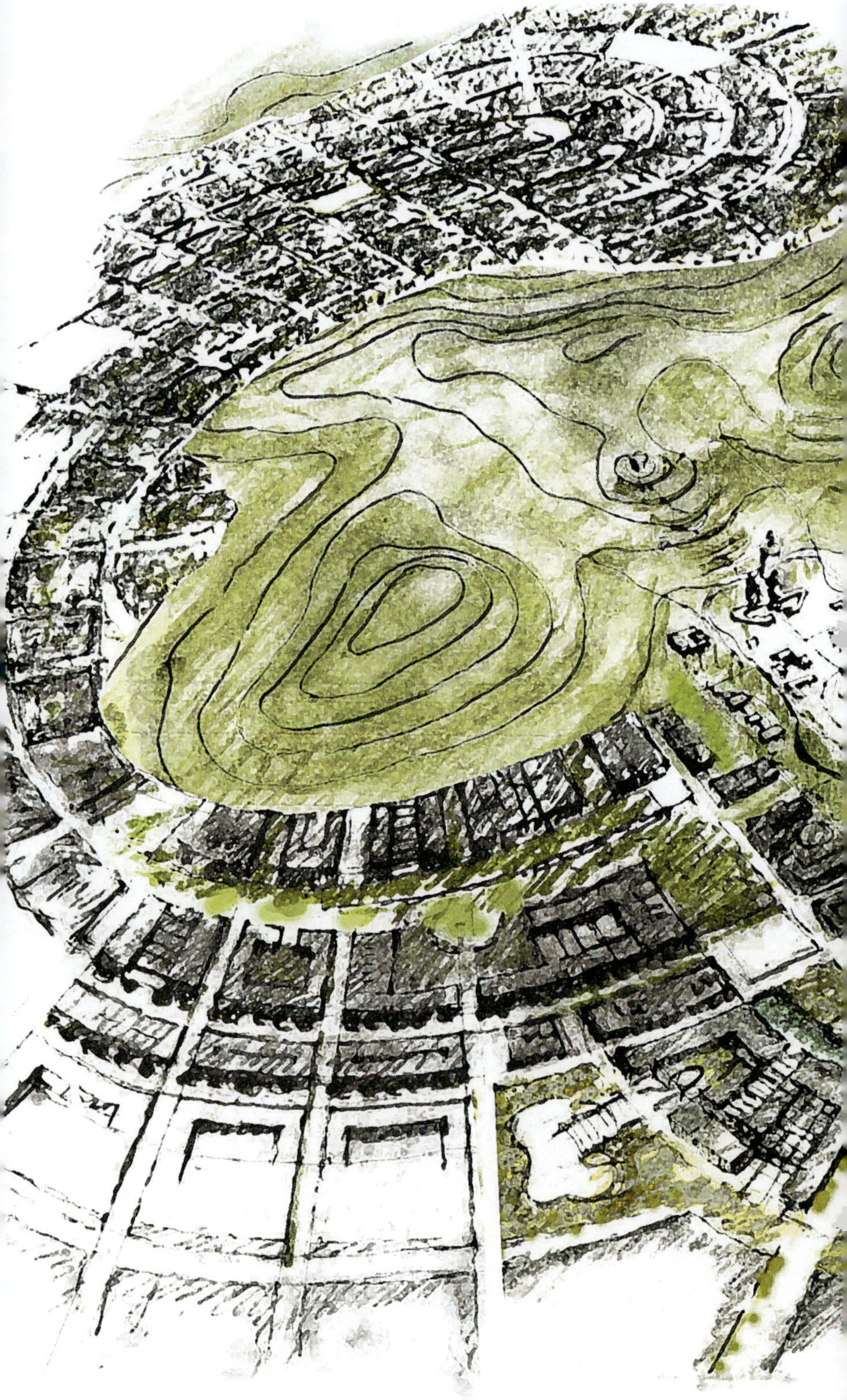

106
Maidar City
Ulaanbaatar, Mongolia, 2016

106
Maidar City
Ulaanbaatar, Mongolia, 2016

The circumstances of tradition, economy and people are perfect to develop the Maidar EcoCity, which will be one of the most advanced urban developments in Asia.

106
Maidar City
Ulaanbaatar, Mongolia, 2016

107
Traffic Business District Core Area
Qingdao, China, 2014

RSAA GmbH

www.rs-aa.com

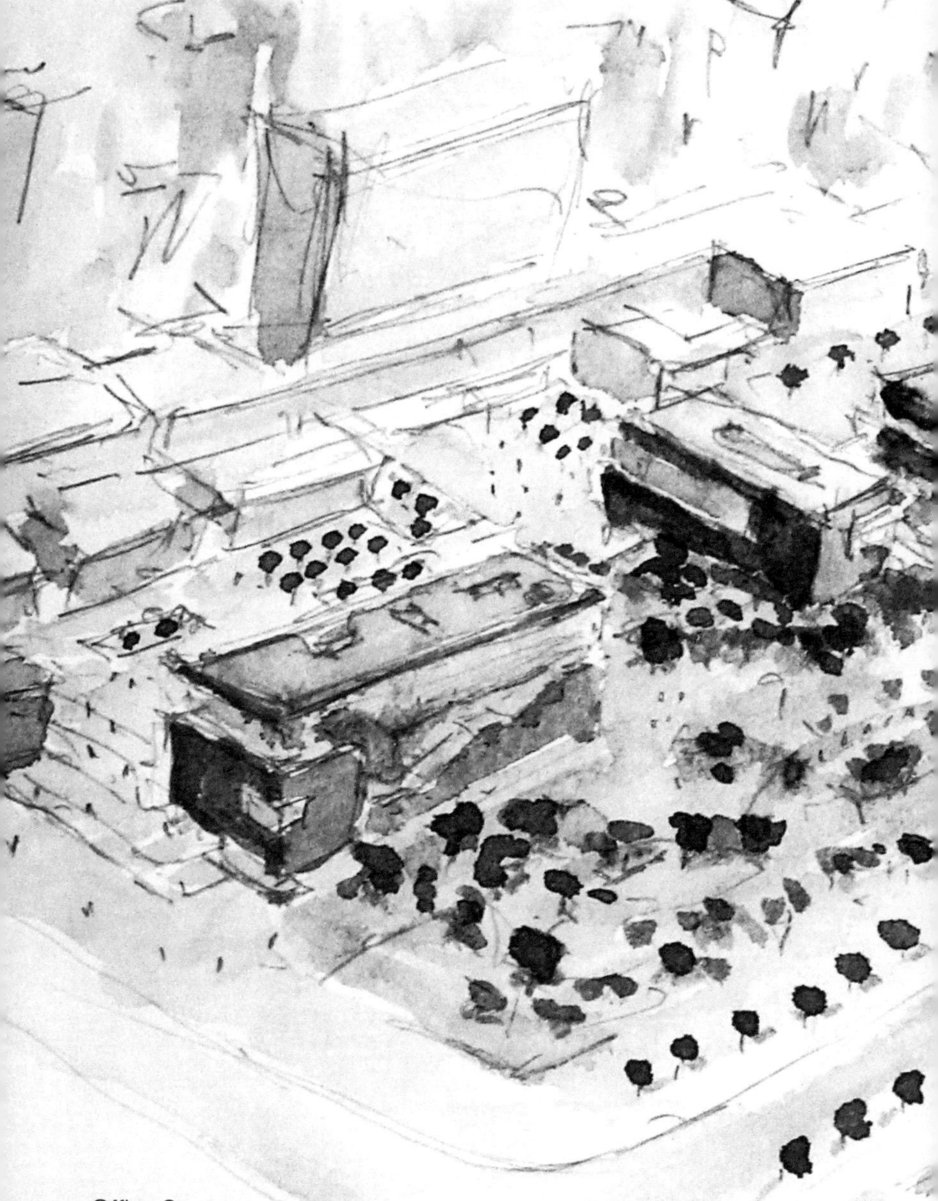

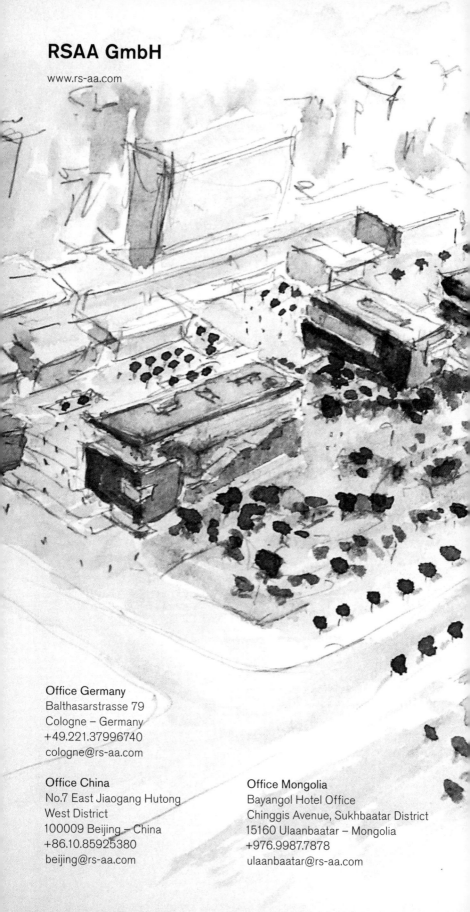

Office Germany
Balthasarstrasse 79
Cologne – Germany
+49.221.37996740
cologne@rs-aa.com

Office China
No.7 East Jiaogang Hutong
West District
100009 Beijing – China
+86.10.85925380
beijing@rs-aa.com

Office Mongolia
Bayangol Hotel Office
Chinggis Avenue, Sukhbaatar District
15160 Ulaanbaatar – Mongolia
+976.9987.7878
ulaanbaatar@rs-aa.com

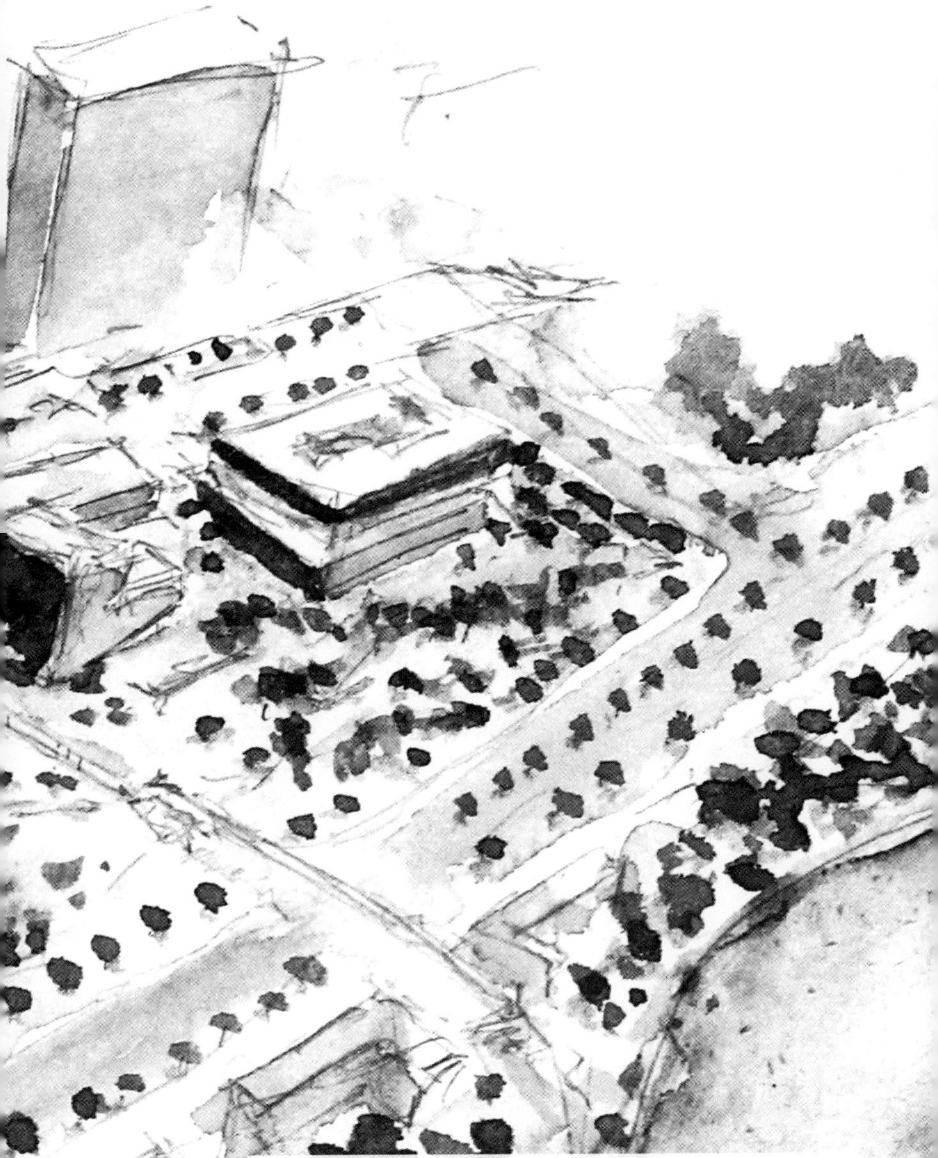

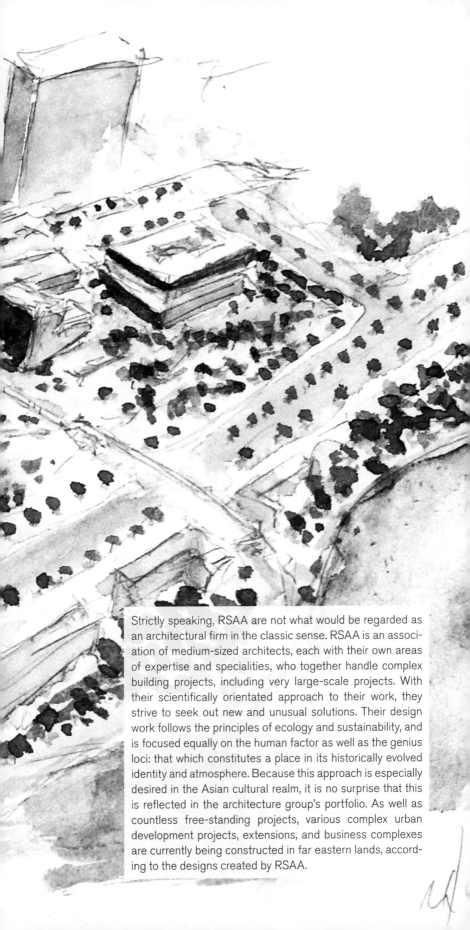

Strictly speaking, RSAA are not what would be regarded as an architectural firm in the classic sense. RSAA is an association of medium-sized architects, each with their own areas of expertise and specialities, who together handle complex building projects, including very large-scale projects. With their scientifically orientated approach to their work, they strive to seek out new and unusual solutions. Their design work follows the principles of ecology and sustainability, and is focused equally on the human factor as well as the genius loci: that which constitutes a place in its historically evolved identity and atmosphere. Because this approach is especially desired in the Asian cultural realm, it is no surprise that this is reflected in the architecture group's portfolio. As well as countless free-standing projects, various complex urban development projects, extensions, and business complexes are currently being constructed in far eastern lands, according to the designs created by RSAA.

schneider+schumacher
Frankfurt am Main

108

Fronius research and development centre

Thalheim, Austria, 2011

A new research and development centre was built at Thalheim, in Austria for a technology business company, which is internationally active. The complex of buildings was developed in accordance with the rural nature of the site. Its three storeys do not rise above the small, tranquil town, but instead seek to form a connection to the rural environment and landscape. The modest, clearly contoured buildings, with their transparent façade design with horizontal emphasis, are unmistakably related to the industrial design of the classical modern architecture. Also, the interior does not belie the fact that the client is an innovative industrial enterprise. The sober, almost cool design corresponds to the incorruptible practicality and rationality of the research work that is carried out here.

Photo: Kirsten Bucher

109
Teda High School
Tianjin, China, 2017

Sustainability is permanent and beautiful. Simplicity and perfection, discipline and creativity, economy and memorable images: these are no contradictions, but components of good architecture.

110
Hager Service Center
Emmenbrücke, Switzerland, 2014

Photo: Jörg Hempel

111
Justice Centre
Shenzhen, China, 2020

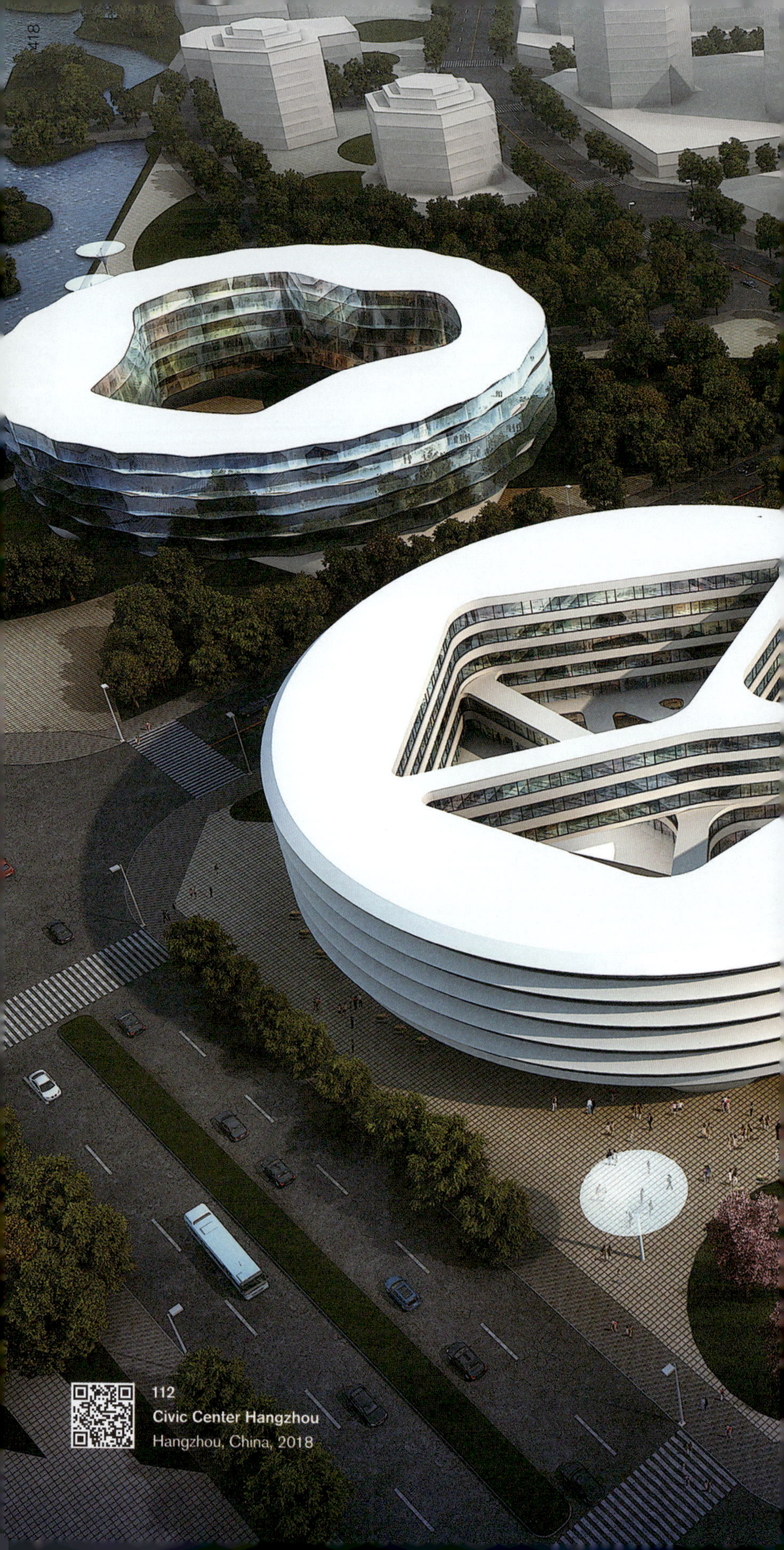

112
Civic Center Hangzhou
Hangzhou, China, 2018

113
Podhagskygasse
Vienna, Austria, 2014

Photo: Jörg Hempel

schneider+schumacher

Good architecture is nothing more than the perfect solution to a particular architectural task; but also nothing less. The quest for that one correct design is the unifying factor in all projects of the company schneider+schumacher, based in Frankfurt, Vienna, and Tianjin. Irrespective of size, this firm of architects, active worldwide, has a portfolio that spans the entire spectrum of planning: product design, residential and specialist construction, cultural institutions, churches, administration and commercial architecture, plus complex urban development projects. Since being founded in 1988, this architectural practice has grown into a business that offers the complete execution of even the largest construction projects, at home and abroad, all from the one source. They have a business unit that deals solely with the development of innovative, sustainable building technology, which is integrated into their planning work, therefore providing a new creative impulse to the designs themselves.

Office Frankfurt am Main
Poststrasse 20 A
60329 Frankfurt am Main – Germany
+49.69.25626262
office@schneider-schumacher.de
www.schneider-schumacher.de

Office Vienna
Schwedenplatz 2/24
1010 Vienna – Austria
+43.1.8905260
office@schneider-schumacher.at
www.schneider-schumacher.at

Office Tianjin
Dagunan Road,
Henghua Building No. 2, Room 908,
300202 Tianjin – China
+86.22.58191890
office@schneider-schumacher.cn
www.schneider-schumacher.cn

Photo: Kirsten Bucher

Spacial Solutions International
Munich

114

Kigali Convention Complex

Kigali, Rwanda, 2016

The dome, with its 38 m-high spiral construction, is the heart of this congress and convention centre in the capital of the east African country Rwanda. With this convention centre, planned by Spacial Solutions International, Kigali has not only received a modern, multifunctional urban quarter, but also a place in which this country's successful political and social change is taking shape. In many respects, the Kigali Convention Center's architecture fulfils the great expectations that were held of it. The striking building, enthroned on a hill, complements the area that is organised as a campus, which includes a new cosmopolitan IT services and office park, plus a five star-hotel with generous event and conference facilities. Its arena offers space for 2,800 people. The convention centre's spectacular roof construction, with its delicate, dynamically ascending spiral pattern, references the country's tradition of circular buildings. With a diameter of 60 m, it straddles the arena in the manner of a hood that is light as a feather.

YOUR AIRFREIGHT
&

114
Kigali Convention Complex
Kigali, Rwanda, 2016

115

House Wessling

Wessling, Germany, 2013

Photo: Atelier Palladium

116

STIHL Qingdao

Qingdao, China, 2013

Photo: Roland Dieterle

117

Headquarters Siegle + Epple

Stuttgart-Weilimdorf, Germany, 2010

Photo: Atelier Altenkirch

At Spacial Solutions International our experience has been in thoroughly researching local and traditional customs and cultures in order to create totally new authentic experiences.

118
Neckarbogen Building
Tübingen, Germany, 2016

Prof. Roland Dieterle

Photo: Myrzik und Jarisch

Spacial Solutions International GmbH

Spacial Solutions International is an architectural practice that tackles complex building projects in Europe, Asia, and Africa. The self-conception of the 20-strong team is based on partnering and interdisciplinary exchange. Joint work on the designs, plans, and projects characterises the company's relationship to clients and partners. In their role as lead consultants, Spacial Solutions International cooperate with leading German engineering firms and consultants, from the initial planning stages right up to completion, with the aim of developing sustainable, long-lasting and flexible architecture. During this process, not only does the company sound out environmentally friendly technical opportunities, such as intelligent building automation systems, but also places equal emphasis on cultural and creative options. That this practice, founded in 2005, has been so successfully involved in projects in Germany and abroad is thanks to their approach of cross-cultural project work, which integrates the respective characteristics and traditions of the project site. The range of work undertaken by Spacial Solutions International spans urban development master plans, the construction of residential buildings, hotels, and cultural facilities, plus buildings for large public sectors, and commercial clients.

Brienner Strasse 46
80333 Munich – Germany
+49.89.547265910
info@spacial-solutions-int.com
www.spacial-solutions-int.com

SSF Ingenieure AG
Munich

119 Baku Crystal Hall
Gerkan Marg und Partner
Baku, Azerbaijan, 2012

The 13,500 m² building, designed by the German architectural firm Gerkan Marg und Partner (gmp), offers space for 25,000 visitors, and is equally suited to host sporting events as it is to large cultural events. Thanks to its crystalline form and unusual location on a small peninsula in the Caspian Sea, the hall counts today as a modern landmark of Baku.

Photo: Nüssli International AG

120 Stadsbrug-Nijmegen
Ney Poulissen, Architects and Engineers
Nijmegen, Netherlands, 2014

Photo: Thea van den Heuvel Fotografie

Gardemann

121
Flyover – Viaduto
São Paulo, Brazil, 2013

Jardins
9 de Julho
Morumbi
C. Universitária

122 Bridge over the IJssel
Quist Wintermans Architects
Hanzelijn, Netherlands, 2012

Photo: Florian Schreiber Fotografie

123 Expo Shanghai 2010 German Pavilion
Schmidhuber + Kaindl
Shanghai, China, 2010

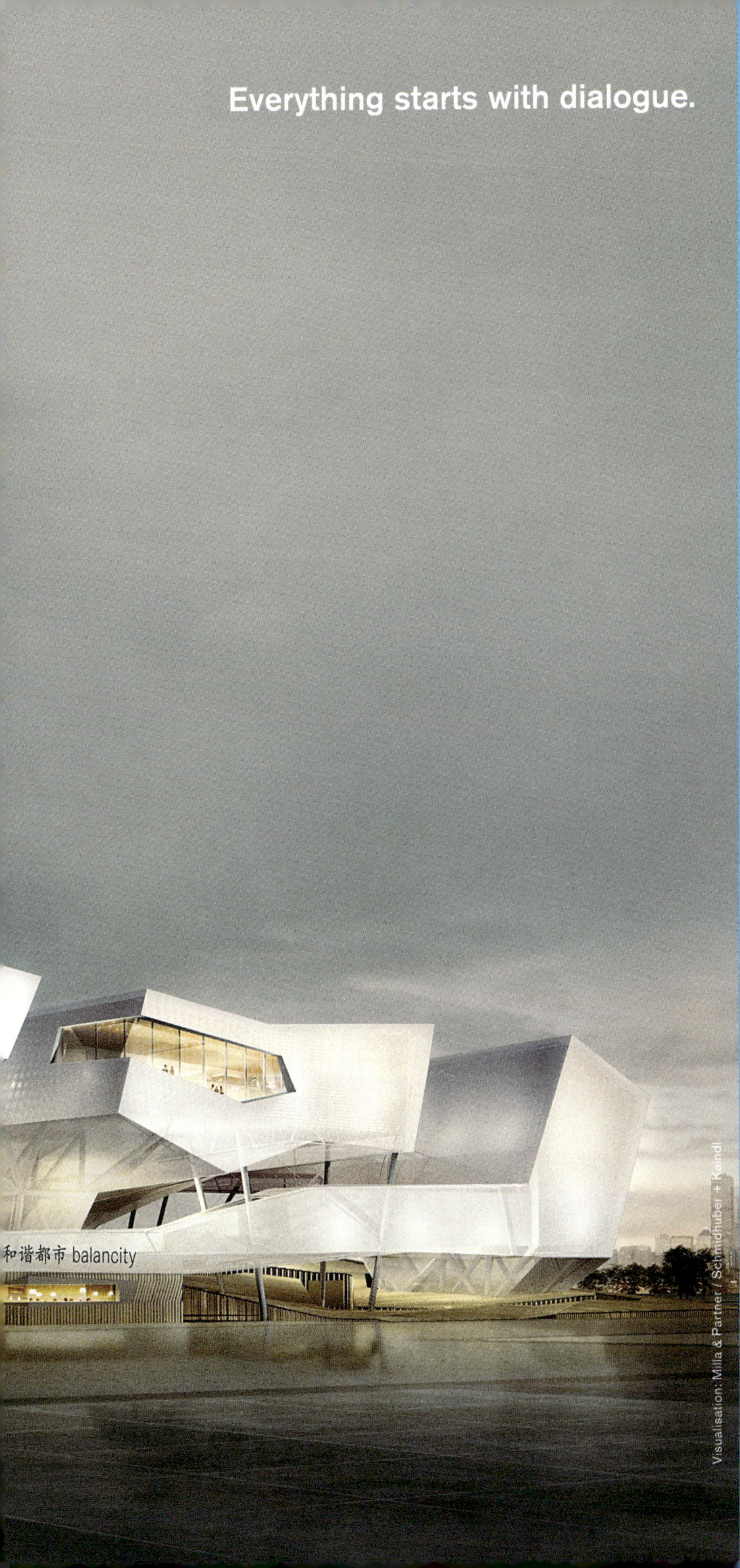
Everything starts with dialogue.
和谐都市 balancity
Visualisation: Milla & Partner / Schmidhuber + Kaindl

124 Expo Milan 2015 German Pavilion
Schmidhuber
Milan, Italy, 2015

Photo: Florian Schreiber Fotografie

BRANDENBURG

SSF Ingenieure AG
Beratende Ingenieure im Bauwesen
Domagkstrasse 1a
80807 Munich – Germany
+49.89.36040-0
muenchen@ssf-ing.de
www.ssf-ing.de
BMZ

Modern architecture requires engineering skills, as the portfolio of the Munich practice SSF Ingenieure attests. Although, 40 years ago, the company's founders regarded themselves purely as designers of supporting structures for bridges, their constantly growing portfolio demonstrates that they are also specialists in complex traffic and high-rise projects. As general planners, the company also handles large urban development and infrastructural building projects throughout the entire world. With its 240 employees, the company founded in 1971 handles not only traffic hubs, airports, and tunnels, but also conference venues, power stations, disposal plants, and special architecture. A special challenge was the Baku Crystal Hall, which was designed and built within just a short period of time for the occasion of the 2012 Eurovision Song Contest being held in the capital of Azerbaijan. As well as planning the supporting structure for the stands and roofing, SSF Ingenieure were also responsible for the foundations and steel structure. As opposed to comparable buildings, the hall was not constructed using the reinforced concrete method, but as a pure steel construction, using prefabricated components.

Staab Architekten

Berlin

125

Ahrenshoop Museum of Art

Ahrenshoop, Germany, 2013

The Ahrenshoop Museum of Art on the Baltic sea island of Darss similarly seeks a link to the site's history. This new building provides the colony of artists based here with a permanent home for the first time, and blends into the historical surroundings in this old fishing village. This new ensemble, comprising a series of interlinked buildings with gabled roofs, displays a definite affinity with the thatched houses in the neighbourhood. But it is no throwback. With its unusual façade design, this modern addition differentiates itself markedly from its surrounding environment. The entire outer shell, including the roof, is made with sheet brass, which shimmers in different colours according to the time of day and position of sun, and will patinate over the course of time.

Photo: Stefan Müller

125
Ahrenshoop Museum of Art
Ahrenshoop, Germany, 2013

Photo: Stefan Müller

Photo: Marcus Ebener

126
Richard Wagner Museum
Bayreuth, Germany, 2015

126

Richard Wagner Museum

Bayreuth, Germany, 2015

Photo: Marcus Ebener

127
LWL-Museum for Art and Culture
Münster, Germany, 2013

Photo: Marcus Ebener

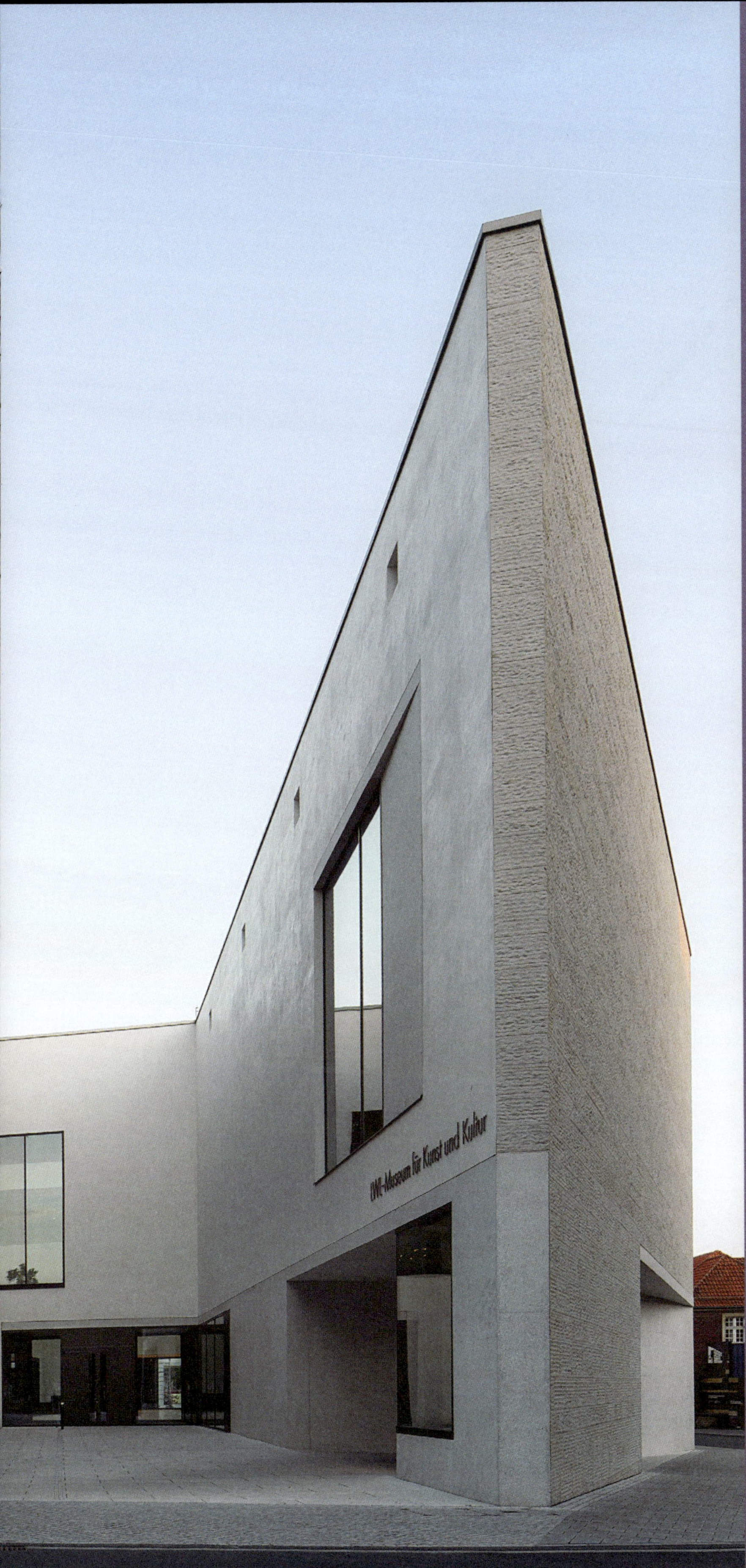
LWL-Museum für Kunst und Kultur

Our strategy of using the cultural, regional, functional, and economic conditions of a project to generate a simple yet specific form, is applicable irrespective of country boundaries.

Photo: Marcus Ebener

127
LWL-Museum for Art and Culture
Münster, Germany, 2013

Staab Architekten GmbH

Schlesische Strasse 27
10997 Berlin – Germany
+49.30.617914-0
info@staab-architekten.com
www.staab-architekten.com

To compress complex architectural conditions into a simple, surprisingly plausible form – that is the approach taken by this Berlin practice, founded in 1991, the company's broad range of building projects spans from new construction in sensitive urban and rural settings to conversions and reinterpretations of listed buildings. The new construction of the LWL Museum for Art and Culture succeeding in complementing the historical buildings in Münster's Domplatz in harmonious fashion. The façade uses treated natural stone, as this characterises the buildings in and around the prominent cathedral square. The new museum opens outwards with an inviting gesture. A sequence of four public rooms, whose character reproduces the noble order of forecourt, entrance courtyard, patio and foyer, places the building into context of the surrounding historical city.

Photo: Zuzanna Kałużna

Index of Architects

The digits refer to the page number.

AS+P Albert Speer + Partner GmbH 25
Auer Weber 41
Bollinger + Grohmann Ingenieure 57
Braun Schlockermann Dreesen 73
Eike Becker_Architekten 89
Eller + Eller Architekten 105
Falk von Tettenborn Architekten 121
Gerber Architekten 137
GRAFT Architekten 153
HPP Architects 169
HWP Planungsgesellschaft mbH 185
ISA Internationales Stadtbauatelier 201
K+P Architekten 217
KSP Jürgen Engel Architekten 233
LAVA Laboratory for Visionary Architecture 249
Meuser Architekten GmbH 265
Nattler Architekten 281
Nickl & Partner Architekten AG 297
OBERMEYER 313
ORANGE BLU building solutions 329
[phase eins]. 345
Rainer Schmidt Landschaftsarchitekten 361
RhineScheme GmbH 377
RSAA Sustainable Architecture and Urban Design 393
schneider+schumacher 409
Spacial Solutions International 425
SSF Ingenieure 441
Staab Architekten 457

Index of Locations

The digits refer to the project number.

Austria
- Thalheim ... 108
- Vienna ... 010, 086, 113

Azerbaijan
- Baku ... 119

Brazil
- São Paulo ... 121

Chile
- Antofagasta ... 007

China
- Beijing ... 063, 104
- Changsha ... 064
- Guangzhou ... 091
- Hangzhou ... 070, 098, 102, 112
- Jining City ... 105
- Lijiang ... 053
- Qingdao ... 065, 107, 116
- Shanghai ... 004, 123
- Shenzhen ... 111
- Tianjin ... 066, 101, 109
- Wuhan ... 103

Croatia
- Split ... 020
- Zagreb ... 021

Czech Republic
- Pilsen ... 088

Dominican Republic
- Santo Domingo ... 029

France
- Antibes ... 006
- Courchevel ... 008
- Grenoble ... 085
- Lens ... 012
- Villeneuve d'Ascq ... 005

Georgia
- Tbilisi ... 092

Germany
- Ahrenshoop ... 125
- Bad Friedrichshall ... 049
- Bayreuth ... 126
- Berlin ... 025, 036, 039, 041, 068
- Bonn ... 022, 081
- Burghaslach ... 076
- Dortmund ... 080
- Dresden ... 050
- Düsseldorf ... 043, 046
- Essen ... 079
- Frankfurt am Main ... 002, 009, 018, 045, 084
- Hamburg ... 031
- Karlsruhe ... 052
- Ludwigshafen ... 023
- Munich ... 030, 057–061, 095, 097
- Münster ... 127
- Neuss ... 019
- Neustadt an der Donau ... 089
- Sankt Augustin ... 040
- Singen ... 082
- Solingen ... 044
- Stuttgart ... 096, 117
- Tübingen ... 118
- Ulm ... 083
- Wessling ... 115
- Wolfsburg ... 038

Haiti
Pétion-Ville 028

Iraq
Baghdad 054

Italy
Milan 124

Kazakhstan
Almaty 013, 075
Astana 073

Luxemburg
Dudelang 056

Mali
Bamako 077

Mongolia
Ulaanbaatar 106

Netherlands
Den Haag 093, 094
Eindhoven 072
Hanzelijn 122
Nijmegen 120

Qatar
Doha 099

Russia
Perm 014
Skolkovo 024
St. Petersburg 015–017, 100
Tjumen 026
Volgograd 027

Rwanda
Kigali 114

Saudi Arabia
Al Khobar 069
Mecca 034
Riyadh 001, 003, 011, 032, 033, 035, 067
Taif 055

Serbia
Belgrade 037

South Korea
Seoul 042

Switzerland
Emmenbrücke 110
Vevey 051

Tanzania
Kigoma 062
Shinyanga 062
Sumbawanga 062
Tabora 062

Turkey
Istanbul 047, 048

Turkmenistan
Ashgabat 078

United Arab Emirates
Abu Dhabi 071, 087

USA
New York City 074

Uzbekistan
Tashkent 090

The Deutsche Nationalbibliothek lists this publication in the Deutsche Nationalbibliografie; detailed bibliographic data are available at http://dnb.d-nb.de

ISBN 978-3-86922-176-2

DOM publishers

© 2016 by DOM publishers, Berlin / Germany
www.dom-publishers.com

This work is subject to copyright. All rights reserved. No part of this publication may be reproduced, stored in a retrieval system, or transferred, in any form or by any means, electronic, mechanical, photocopying, recording, or otherwise, without the prior written permission of the publishers. Sources and owners of rights are stated to the best of our knowledge; please signal any we might have omitted.

Editorial Directors
Gabriele Seitz, Melanie Läge

Author
Cornelia Dörries

Proofreading
Laura Thépot

QR Codes
Christoph Gößmann

Design
Masako Tomokiyo

Printing
Tiger Printing (Hong Kong) Co., Ltd.
www.tigerprinting.hk

Picture Credits
Unless otherwise indicated, photos, plans, visualisations and other graphics were supplied from the respective architectural practices.

NAX NETWORK FOR ARCHITECTURE EXCHANGE

DW Deutsche Welle

Contemporary Architecture
Made in Germany
Europe

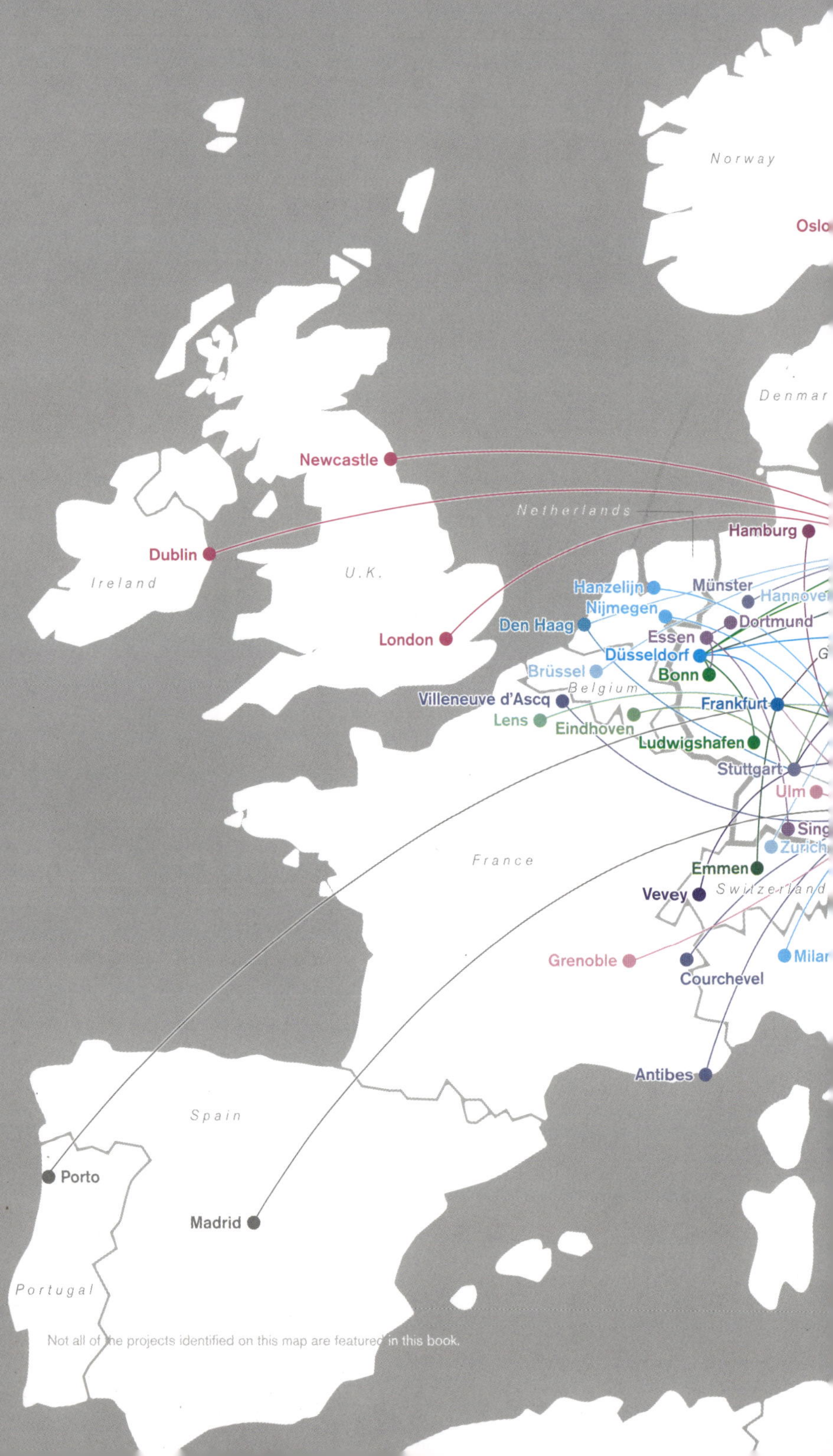

Not all of the projects identified on this map are featured in this book.